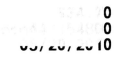

CONSTITUTIONAL
AMENDMENTS
BEYOND THE BILL OF RIGHTS

Amendment XXV
Presidential Disability
and Succession

Other Books of Related Interest

Opposing Viewpoints Series

American Values

Civil Liberties

Political Campaigns

The U.S. Supreme Court

Current Controversies Series

Federal Elections

The U.S. Economy

CONSTITUTIONAL
AMENDMENTS
BEYOND THE BILL OF RIGHTS

Amendment XXV
Presidential Disability
and Succession

Sylvia Engdahl, Book Editor

GREENHAVEN PRESS
A part of Gale, Cengage Learning

GALE
CENGAGE Learning™

Detroit • New York • San Francisco • New Haven, Conn • Waterville, Maine • London

GALE
CENGAGE Learning™

Christine Nasso, *Publisher*
Elizabeth Des Chenes, *Managing Editor*

© 2010 Greenhaven Press, a part of Gale, Cengage Learning.

Gale and Greenhaven Press are registered trademarks used herein under license.

For more information, contact:
Greenhaven Press
27500 Drake Rd.
Farmington Hills, MI 48331-3535
Or you can visit our Internet site at gale.cengage.com

For product information and technology assistance, contact us at

Gale Customer Support, 1-800-877-4253
For permission to use material from this text or product, submit all requests online at www.cengage.com/permissions

Further permissions questions can be emailed to permissionrequest@cengage.com

Articles in Greenhaven Press anthologies are often edited for length to meet page requirements. In addition, original titles of these works are changed to clearly present the main thesis and to explicitly indicate the author's opinion. Every effort is made to ensure that Greenhaven Press accurately reflects the original intent of the authors. Every effort has been made to trace the owners of copyrighted material.

Cover photograph © Bettmann/Corbis.

LIBRARY OF CONGRESS CATALOGING-IN-PUBLICATION DATA

Amendment XXV : presidential disability and succession / Sylvia Engdahl, book editor.
    p. cm. -- (Constitutional amendments: beyond the Bill of Rights)
    Includes bibliographical references and index.
    ISBN 978-0-7377-4698-3 (hardcover) -- ISBN 978-0-7377-5111-6 (pbk.)
    1. Presidents--Succession--United States--History. 2. United States. Constitution. 25th Amendment. I. Engdahl, Sylvia. II. Title: Amendment 25. III. Title: Amendment Twenty five.
    KF5082.A85 2010
    342.73'062--dc22
                                                                2010003701

Printed in the United States of America
1 2 3 4 5 6 7 14 13 12 11 10

Contents

Chapter 1: History of the Twenty-fifth Amendment

An assistant U.S. attorney general argues in 1959 that although in the past prolonged uncertainty about what powers the vice president could exercise in case of presidential disability was tolerable, in the age of nuclear weapons it is not, and a constitutional amendment to clarify this issue is needed.

Chapter 2: The Twenty-fifth Amendment in Action

The Twenty-fifth Amendment was used for the first time in 1973 when Vice President Spiro Agnew resigned in the face of criminal charges of tax fraud and President Richard Nixon appointed Gerald Ford to replace him.

Chapter 3: Limitations of the Twenty-fifth Amendment

Law professors point out that the Twenty-fifth Amendment does not address a situation in which the vice president is disabled or there is no vice president at the time the president becomes disabled. The amendment also does not cover the possibility of the death or disability of either of them after election but before inauguration.

Chapter 4: Solutions to Potential Problems of Presidential Succession and Disability

A report prepared for members of Congress points out that there is controversy about what the Constitution means by the word *officer*, and therefore about whether members of Congress can legally be in the line of succession to the presidency.

A political science professor argues that determination of disability, especially mental disability, requires sustained observation and that periodic examination by a medical advisory commission would increase the likelihood of arbitrary medical judgments and would also undermine the presidential image of strength, thus harming the president's ability to lead.

Appendix

Presidential Disability and Succession

> "Today's Constitution is a realistic docu-
> ment of freedom only because of several
> corrective amendments. Those amend-
> ments speak to a sense of decency and
> fairness."
>
> *Thurgood Marshall*

While the U.S. Constitution forms the backbone of American democracy, the amendments make the Constitution a living, ever-evolving document. Interpretation and analysis of the Constitution inform lively debate in every branch of government, as well as among students, scholars, and all other citizens, and views on various articles of the Constitution have changed over the generations. Formally altering the Constitution, however, can happen only through the amendment process. The Greenhaven Press series The Bill of Rights examines the first ten amendments to the Constitution. Constitutional Amendments: Beyond the Bill of Rights continues the exploration, addressing key amendments ratified since 1791.

The process of amending the Constitution is painstaking. While other options are available, the method used for nearly every amendment begins with a congressional bill that must pass both the Senate and the House of Representatives by a two-thirds majority. Then the amendment must be ratified by three-quarters of the states. Many amendments have been proposed since the Bill of Rights was adopted in 1791, but only seventeen have been ratified.

It may be difficult to imagine a United States where women and African Americans are prohibited from voting, where the federal government allows one human being to enslave another, or where some citizens are denied equal protection under the law. While many of our most fundamental liberties are protected by the Bill of Rights, the amendments that followed have significantly broadened and enhanced the rights of American citizens. Such rights may be taken for granted today, but when the amendments were ratified, many were considered groundbreaking and proved to be explosively controversial.

Each volume in Constitutional Amendments provides an in-depth exploration of an amendment and its impact through primary and secondary sources, both historical and contemporary. Primary sources include landmark Supreme Court rulings, speeches by prominent experts, and newspaper editorials. Secondary sources include historical analyses, law journal articles, book excerpts, and magazine articles. Each volume first presents the historical background of the amendment, creating a colorful picture of the circumstances surrounding the amendment's passage: the campaigns to sway public opinion, the congressional debates, and the struggle for ratification. Next, each volume examines the ways the court system has been used to test the validity of the amendment and addresses the ramifications of the amendment's passage. The final chapter of each volume presents viewpoints that explore current controversies and debates relating to ways in which the amendment affects our everyday lives.

Numerous features are included in each Constitutional Amendments volume:

- An originally written introduction presents a concise yet thorough overview of the amendment.

- A time line provides historical context by describing key events, organizations, and people relating to the ratification of the amendment, subsequent court cases, and the impact of the amendment.

- An annotated table of contents offers an at-a-glance summary of each primary and secondary source essay included in the volume.

- The complete text of the amendment, followed by a "plain English" explanation, brings the amendment into clear focus for students and other readers.

- Graphs, charts, tables, and maps enhance the text.

- A list of all twenty-seven Constitutional Amendments offers quick reference.

- An annotated list of court cases relevant to the amendment broadens the reader's understanding of the judiciary's role in interpreting the Constitution.

- A bibliography of books, periodicals, and Web sites aids readers in further research.

- A detailed subject index allows readers to quickly find the information they need.

With the aid of this series, students and other researchers will become better informed of their rights and responsibilities as American citizens. Constitutional Amendments: Beyond the Bill of Rights examines the roots of American democracy, bringing to life the ways the Constitution has evolved and how it has impacted this nation's history.

Amendment Text and Explanation

The Twenty-fifth Amendment to the United States Constitution

Passed by Congress July 6, 1965. Ratified February 10, 1967.

Section 1.

In case of the removal of the President from office or of his death or resignation, the Vice President shall become President.

Section 2.

Whenever there is a vacancy in the office of the Vice President, the President shall nominate a Vice President who shall take office upon confirmation by a majority vote of both Houses of Congress.

Section 3.

Whenever the President transmits to the President pro tempore of the Senate and the Speaker of the House of Representatives his written declaration that he is unable to discharge the powers and duties of his office, and until he transmits to them a written declaration to the contrary, such powers and duties shall be discharged by the Vice President as Acting President.

Section 4.

Whenever the Vice President and a majority of either the principal officers of the executive departments or of such other body as Congress may by law provide, transmit to the President pro tempore of the Senate and the Speaker of the House of Representatives their written declaration that the President is unable to discharge the powers and duties of his office, the Vice President shall immediately assume the powers and duties of the office as Acting President.

Thereafter, when the President transmits to the President pro tempore of the Senate and the Speaker of the House of Representatives his written declaration that no inability exists, he shall resume the powers and duties of his office unless the Vice President and a majority of either the principal officers of the executive department or of such other body as Congress may by law provide, transmit within four days to the President pro tempore of the Senate and the Speaker of the House of Representatives their written declaration that the President is unable to discharge the powers and duties of his office. Thereupon Congress shall decide the issue, assembling within forty-eight hours for that purpose if not in session. If the Congress, within twenty-one days after receipt of the latter written declaration, or, if Congress is not in session, within twenty-one days after Congress is required to assemble, determines by two-thirds vote of both Houses that the President is unable to discharge the powers and duties of his office, the Vice President shall continue to discharge the same as Acting President; otherwise, the President shall resume the powers and duties of his office.

Explanation

Section 1.

If the president is removed from office by impeachment or dies or resigns, the vice president shall become president.

Section 2.

If the vice president becomes president or is removed from office by impeachment or dies or resigns, the president shall nominate a new vice president, who must be confirmed by a majority vote of both houses of Congress.

Section 3.

If the president sends the president pro tempore of the Senate and the Speaker of the House of Representatives a written notice that he is temporarily unable to exercise the powers and duties of his office, the vice president shall immediately become acting president. To regain his powers and resume his duties the president must send a second written notice to those congressional leaders stating that he is ready and able to return to office.

Section 4.

If the vice president and a majority of the cabinet send the president pro tempore of the Senate and the Speaker of the House of Representatives a written notice that the president is unable to exercise the powers and duties of his office, the vice president shall immediately become acting president. But if the president then sends the president pro tempore of the Senate and the Speaker of the House of Representatives his written declaration that he is not disabled, he shall resume his powers and duties unless the vice president and a majority of the cabinet send a second declaration within four days. If this is done, Congress shall decide the issue, assembling within forty-eight hours for that purpose if not in session. If Congress determines within twenty-one days by a two-thirds majority of both Houses that the president is indeed unable to perform his duties, the vice president shall continue as acting president; otherwise, the president shall resume the powers and duties of his office.

Introduction

"Nothing could have seemed worse than that news from Dallas last November," wrote James MacGregor Burns in the popular magazine *Saturday Evening Post* two months after the 1963 assassination of President John F. Kennedy. "But two things could have been worse for the country: if [Vice President] Lyndon Johnson had been assassinated too; or if John Kennedy had been left alive but mentally disabled. We have gambled too long with the question of presidential disability."

At that time there was no legal provision for what to do if the president were to become disabled. There was not even any clear authorization for what to do if he died, although it had long been the practice for the vice president to become president. The Constitution states only that in such a case the president's powers and duties "devolve upon the vice president," which some in the nineteenth century believed was supposed to mean that the vice president would be merely acting president. In 1841, when President William Henry Harrison died and Vice President John Tyler took over, former president John Quincy Adams wrote in his diary, "I paid a visit this morning to Mr. Tyler, who styles himself President of the United States, and not Vice-President acting as President, which would be the correct style." Congress and the public accepted Tyler as president, however; so a rule that became known as the Tyler Precedent was established.

The ambiguity was nevertheless worrying. The death or disability of a sitting president was not an unusual occurrence: three presidents before Kennedy had been assassinated, four had died in office of natural causes, and several others had been so seriously disabled by illness that the nation was without adequate leadership for a prolonged period. When in 1881 President James A. Garfield was shot by an assassin, he lingered for eighty days while Vice President Chester A. Arthur declined to take action for fear of being labeled a usurper. Woodrow Wilson, who was president during World War I, suffered a stroke in 1919 and was ill for eighteen months, during which much of the country's business was handled by his wife; he never completely recovered. Neither Congress nor the public was told how serious his condition was. Some scholars believe that Wilson's disability was responsible for the failure of the United States to join the League of Nations, which he had conceived and strongly favored but which was opposed by the Senate.

It is now known that a number of other presidents were ill without the public being aware of it. Until fairly recently it was not the custom for people's medical problems to be openly discussed, and no one claimed that citizens had a right to know about their leaders' state of health, as is believed today. For example, Franklin D. Roosevelt—who for many years had served successfully as president without publicly revealing that the aftereffects of poliomyelitis had made him unable to walk—was ill with heart failure and cerebral vascular disease long before he died of a cerebral hemorrhage in 1945. He was ill even at the time of his fourth election to office in 1944, and some maintain that it reduced his ability to deal with foreign leaders during the last months of World War II.

Each time there was a crisis involving a president's illness, the need to plan for future situations was discussed yet Congress took no action. Dismay over the nation's narrow escape from chaos following the shooting of Kennedy was the last straw. By then, the president of the United States was a world leader with the power to launch nuclear weapons; the lack of a competent person in that post for even a few hours could have serious consequences. For this reason, on the day of the assassination, Vice President Lyndon Johnson took the oath of office, and thus became president, aboard Air Force One on the ground in Dallas before taking off for Washington. But

Johnson had had health problems in the past, and the congressional leaders first and second in line to succeed him were old men—one of them was eighty-six. Within a month, Congress, which had already been studying various plans for dealing with presidential inability, began to consider them more seriously and to debate the provisions of a proposed constitutional amendment.

Getting a measure through Congress is a slow process. For a constitutional amendment to be adopted it must, like any bill, be approved by two or more committees, after which it must be passed by both the Senate and the House of Representatives. Senator Birch Bayh, who introduced the resolution that eventually became the Twenty-fifth Amendment, worked hard to gain the support of congressional leaders, but although there was widespread agreement that something needed to be done, working out the details was difficult. There were many conflicting suggestions as to how a new vice president should be chosen when that office was vacant, and the debates about presidential disability involved far more complex issues, such as how to define inability, who should determine when it exists, and how the president could be protected against attempts to remove him wrongly. A resolution setting forth the amendment was passed by the Senate in the fall of 1964, but that was too late for it to be taken up by the House before Congress adjourned, and it therefore expired. A new bill had to be proposed in the next congressional session.

In January 1965 Senator Bayh obtained the support of President Johnson, who mentioned it in his State of the Union address and then sent an official message to Congress urging that the bill be passed. But the arguments grew more intense once it became apparent that the proposed amendment might really make it all the way to passage and then proceed to ratification. Various senators and representatives kept pointing out potential situations that it would not cover. There were long, heated discussions about the precise wording to be used.

Although the most difficult problems to resolve concerned Section 4 of the amendment, which deals with removing a president against his will, at one point late in the negotiations someone went back to the question of a vice presidential vacancy, protesting that members of the House, instead of confirming the president's nominee, might sit on the nomination so that the Speaker of the House would remain first in the line of succession to the presidency. At this, Senator Sam Ervin declared, "God help this nation if we ever get a House of Representatives, or a Senate, which will wait for a president to die so someone they love more than their country will succeed to the presidency."

After the Senate passed the new bill, the House of Representatives insisted on amendments that the Senate would not accept, and the differences had to be worked out by a joint committee. This took up more time. But finally, eighteen months after the initial introduction of the resolution, it was passed and sent to the states. Ratification by the necessary three-quarters of the states took another year and a half. The amendment officially became part of the Constitution on February 10, 1967.

It was not long—only six and a half years, in fact—before a need arose to use the Amendment. Vice President Spiro Agnew resigned after a scandal, leaving that office vacant. For the first time, a president used his power to appoint a new vice president when Richard Nixon nominated Gerald Ford. Ford was vice president for less than a year when President Nixon himself was forced to resign due to his involvement in the Watergate scandal, and Ford succeeded to the presidency, appointing Nelson Rockefeller as the new vice president to follow him. This smooth transition of power after the scandals that preceded it made the nation feel greatly relieved by the fact that the Constitution worked; however, some argued that the Twenty-fifth Amendment did not work, for the congressional confirmation of Rockefeller took a long time, during which there was no vice president in office.

Section 3 of the Twenty-fifth Amendment, which permits the president to turn his power over to the vice president temporarily if he is unable to carry out his duties, has been used three times: President Ronald Reagan, and twice President George W. Bush, underwent medical procedures that required anesthesia. These were brief periods of time, only a few hours, but it was deemed important to have someone with presidential powers available in case of a national emergency.

There has never been a need to use Section 4 of the amendment, which provides for a case when a president is too seriously disabled to voluntarily relinquish his power. It was known when the amendment was written that it would not cover all the potential scenarios of this kind. Senator Bayh and its other supporters believed that if it attempted to do so, it would become so complicated that it would not be possible to reach enough agreement for it to pass. So debates have continued, and still continue, about who should determine when a president is disabled and what evidence should be required. No vice president of the United States has ever sought to grab power, but since it is not inconceivable that this might happen in the future, some believe the amendment needs clarification. Others think that a system for objectively judging the president's health could be established without any constitutional change.

Many experts feel that the most immediate problem concerns what would happen if both the president and vice president—and perhaps others in the line of succession—were killed at the same time. This was not considered when the Twenty-fifth Amendment was adopted, as it would have been thought extremely unlikely, but since the terrorist attacks of September 11, 2001, it has been recognized as a potentially disastrous possibility. The amendment does not specify the line of succession; there is merely a provision in the original Constitution for succession to be established by Congress. But some feel that the Constitution should be further amended to allow the inclusion of people in the line of succession such as state governors who live and work outside Washington, D.C.

The Twenty-fifth Amendment has never been the subject of a court case. The Supreme Court has briefly cited it in several unrelated cases to illustrate the meaning of certain terminology or the importance of the presidency, but no one has disputed its interpretation, nor is anyone likely to. As law professor Peter M. Shane said in a blog criticizing its fictional use in an episode of the TV series *24*, "To get the Twenty-Fifth Amendment right, all you need do is to read it."

Chronology

1963

On November 22 President John F. Kennedy is assassinated. The nation is dismayed by the realization that if he had survived but had been mentally disabled, there would have been no way for the vice president to take over the duties of president. Vice President Lyndon Johnson succeeds Kennedy, leaving a vacancy in the office of vice president.

On December 12 Senator Birch Bayh of Indiana introduces a resolution in the Senate proposing a constitutional amendment to deal with presidential succession and disability.

1964

On January 17 the Senate resolution is referred to the Subcommittee on Constitutional Amendments. Between January 22 and March 5, the subcommittee holds hearings on the resolution.

On May 27, after some revision, the resolution is referred to the Senate Judiciary Committee.

On August 4 the resolution is unanimously approved by the Senate Judiciary Committee.

On September 29 the resolution is passed in the Senate by a vote of 65 to 0.

On October 3 Congress adjourns without having taken any further action on the resolution. This means the resolution dies and must be introduced again when the new Congress convenes.

1965

On January 4 a resolution equivalent to the one that passed the previous Senate is introduced in the House of Representatives. On January 6 a corresponding resolution is introduced in the new Senate.

On January 20 President Johnson is inaugurated for a full term, and Hubert Humphrey, his running mate in the 1964 presidential election, becomes vice president; thus that office is no longer vacant.

On January 29 the Senate Subcommittee on Constitutional Amendments holds new hearings on the resolution.

On February 1 the resolution is favorably reported to the Senate Judiciary Committee, and on February 4 that committee reports favorably on it to the Senate.

Between February 7 and February 17 the House Judiciary Committee holds hearings on the corresponding resolution.

On February 19 the Senate resolution passes by a vote of 72 to 0. On February 22 it is delivered to the House of Representatives.

On April 13 the House of Representatives passes the Senate resolution, in modified form, by a vote of 368 to 29.

On April 22 the resolution is returned to the Senate, which disagrees with the House amendments.

Between May 11 and June 10, a joint committee considers the resolution.

On June 30 the joint committee's report is passed by the House of Representatives and delivered to the Senate.

On July 6 the Senate passes the joint report by a vote of 68 to 5. The proposed amendment is sent to the states for ratification.

On July 12 Nebraska becomes the first state to ratify the amendment. However, the governor does not sign it until the next day, after Wisconsin has ratified it, so there is doubt about which state is legally first.

1967

On February 10 Minnesota and Nevada become the thirty-seventh and thirty-eighth states, respectively, to ratify the amendment, thereby incorporating it into the Constitution.

On February 23 at a White House ceremony, the Twenty-fifth Amendment is officially proclaimed to be in effect.

1973

On October 12, after Vice President Spiro Agnew's resignation, the Twenty-fifth Amendment is used for the first time when President Richard Nixon nominates Gerald Ford to the vice presidency.

On December 6 Ford's nomination is confirmed by Congress, and he becomes vice president.

1974

On August 9, after President Richard Nixon's resignation, Gerald Ford becomes president.

On August 20 President Ford nominates Nelson Rockefeller to fill the vacancy of the vice presidency.

On December 19, after a lengthy congressional hearing, Rockefeller's nomination is confirmed, and he becomes vice president.

1981

On March 30 President Ronald Reagan is shot during an assassination attempt. Although he is seriously injured and requires emergency surgery, the Twenty-fifth Amendment is not invoked, and many later believe that it should have been.

1985

On July 13 President Reagan undergoes a planned surgery and temporarily turns his power over to Vice President George H.W. Bush, using the procedure prescribed by the Twenty-fifth Amendment but not officially invoking it.

1988

The Miller Commission on Presidential Disability and the Twenty-Fifth Amendment, which was formed in 1985 by the Miller Center for Public Affairs at the University of Virginia and cochaired by the amendment's principal author, Birch Bayh, issues a report urging that written guidelines for the application of its disability provisions be put into place before the inauguration of the next president.

1993

In January the Working Group on Presidential Disability, composed of about fifty physicians, lawyers, and other experts, is formed in response to former president Jimmy Carter's concerns about serious deficiencies in the Twenty-fifth Amendment.

1996

In December the Working Group on Presidential Disability presents its recommendations to President Bill Clinton. Its consensus is that although the Twenty-fifth Amendment does not cover all contingencies, no amendment could, and that formal plans should be made for implementing its disability provisions.

2002

On June 29 President George W. Bush undergoes a medical procedure requiring anesthesia, and Vice President Dick Cheney briefly becomes acting president.

2003

In September a joint congressional committee holds hearings to discuss the problems of presidential succession made evident by the terrorist attacks of September 11, 2001.

2007

In January a bill, H.R. 540, to expand the line of presidential succession is introduced into Congress, but it never gets out of committee and thus is not acted on before the 110th Congress adjourns.

On July 21 Vice President Cheney again becomes acting president while President Bush undergoes a medical procedure requiring anesthesia.

2009

In June the Continuity of Government Commission, a privately funded group composed of members with experience in various branches of government, publishes its report *The Continuity of the Presidency*, which is concerned with what would happen in case of a catastrophic attack on Washington, D.C.

History of the Twenty-fifth Amendment

Presidential Disability Should Be Dealt with by Law, Not Amendment of the Constitution

Harry S. Truman

Harry S. Truman was the thirty-third president of the United States, serving from 1945 to 1953. In the following article, which he wrote several years after leaving office, he argues that a process should be established to deal with a situation in which a president becomes incapacitated. In his opinion, to write this into the Constitution would not provide enough flexibility. He recommends that when the president is unable to perform the duties of his office, a committee composed of representatives from the three branches of government should select a board of medical authorities to decide whether the incapacitation is permanent. If it is, Congress should have the power to declare that the vice president is president, and he should then serve out the full term of his predecessor. Truman asserts that once a president is relieved of his office he should not be entitled to return to it.

There has been an understanding reluctance to deal with the delicate and sensitive problem of what we are to do when any President becomes incapacitated and is unable to perform his duties. Our Founding Fathers did not provide for such an eventuality. During the 168 years of our history under the Constitution there have been only two occasions when the question arose of a President's ability to serve. I refer to James A. Garfield and Woodrow Wilson. We have been fortunate, indeed, that we have not had to face such crises more often.

But the job of the President is getting to be an almost unendurable mental and physical burden, and we ought not to go on trusting to luck to see us through.

Harry S. Truman, "Truman Proposes a Panel On a President's Disability," *The New York Times,* June 24, 1957, pp. 13–15. Copyright © 1957 by The New York Times Company. Reproduced by permission.

We may find that we have waited too long to provide a way of meeting the situation in the event a President becomes incapacitated. There have been suggestions to deal with the matter through legislation. Others have proposed amending the Constitution.

The Constitution Should Remain Flexible

However we deal with it eventually, this is too vital a matter to be acted on hastily without the widest discussion and study. I have felt that there is always great danger in writing too much into the Constitution. We must have certain flexibility to meet changing conditions. We have already experienced the consequences of hastily amending the Constitution without adequate public discussion, as in the cases of the 18th and 22d amendments (prohibition and limiting any President to two terms).

In response to the many letters I have received on the subject from all parts of the country and the world, I am taking the liberty of suggesting a way to meet this problem.

I would like to make it perfectly clear that it is not my intention to cast reflections on anyone, or to raise any doubts about the health or condition of the President. Along with all of our citizens, I wish him good health and a long life.

But there is a growing concern about our needs to provide against the danger of a lapse in the functioning of the Presidency and the crises that might ensue.

The power of the President of the United States and his influence on the world today have grown so great that his well-being is of paramount interest to people everywhere. It is no longer a matter to be decided by political leaders and constitutional authorities.

Even a minor indisposition of the President will set into motion unexpected and often unreasoning fears. . . .

Serving as the thirty-third president of the United States, Harry S. Truman believed that presidential succession should not be written into the Constitution by amendment as it would not provide enough flexibility. MPI/Hulton Archive/Getty Images.

Role of President Has Changed

The framers of our Constitution drafted a brilliant and inspired document in which they anticipated and provided for nearly all of the basic developments of our democracy. But who could fully foresee the role of the American Presidency in the kind of a world in which we now live—a role which also requires the President to be available in person at any hour to make decisions which he alone can make and which cannot be put off?

As Vice President, I found myself acutely conscious of this problem in a personal way when I met President [Franklin D.] Roosevelt upon his return from Yalta. Up to that time I regarded the circumstances of an incapacitated President as an academic problem in history, such as was posed by Presidents Garfield and Wilson.

After the first shock of seeing President Roosevelt, I tried to dismiss from my mind the ominous thoughts of a possible breakdown, counting on his ability to bounce back from the strains and stress of office. After Yalta, President Roosevelt continued to carry on with sustained energy and alertness—until suddenly called by death.

From the day I succeeded to the Presidency, I have been thinking about the needs of an act of legislation to provide machinery to meet the emergency of a President's disability.

Successor from Congress Not Cabinet

Shortly after taking office, I considered setting up a commission to study the problem and make recommendations. But in the midst of war and during the period of postwar reconstruction we were preoccupied with more immediate and urgent matters.

I therefore chose instead to recommend to the Congress a change by statute of succession to the Presidency from the Cabinet to the Congress in the event the nation was without a Vice President. Up to that time the Secretary of State was next in order of succession.

I did not think that a Cabinet officer—who is not elected by the people—should succeed to the Presidency, which is an elective office. The Speaker of the House who is, in fact, the top ranking elected public official, after the President and Vice President, is now, under the new law, next in succession.

This, however, does not meet the problem when a President is unable to perform the duties of his office.

A Committee Should Decide

I suggest, therefore, that the following proposal may provide us with a workable solution:

1. When a President is stricken with an illness, raising the question of his ability to carry out the duties of his office, there should come into being a committee of 7 composed of representatives of the 3 branches of the Government. This committee should consist of the Vice President, the Chief Justice of the United States, the Speaker of the House, and the majority and minority leaders of both the House of Representatives and the Senate.

This committee would select a board of leading medical authorities drawn from top medical schools of the nation. This medical board, thus chosen, would then make the necessary examinations, presenting its finding to the committee of seven. Should the finding of the medical board indicate that the President is unable to perform his duties, and that he is, in fact, truly incapacitated and not merely stricken with a transitory illness, then the committee of seven would so inform the Congress.

Congress then would have the right to act, and by a two-thirds vote of the full membership declare the Vice President as President.

The Vice President, designated as President, would thereupon serve out the full term of his predecessor. Should the stricken President, thus relieved, experience during this term a complete recovery, he would not be entitled to repossess the office.

Should the Congress be in adjournment or recess when a President is incapacitated, the Vice President, the Speaker and Chief Justice should call a meeting of the committee of seven. This committee, after receiving the medical findings, would have authority to call Congress into special session for the purpose of declaring the Vice President as President.

It Is Not Necessary to Amend the Constitution to Resolve Presidential Disability Questions

David Fellman

David Fellman was a political science professor at the University of Wisconsin when he authored the following viewpoint, which is from a letter he wrote in reply to a questionnaire he received from a congressional committee that was studying presidential disability. He states that disability was not defined in the Constitution and that he does not believe it should be defined in legislation. In his opinion the law should be clear that if a president who is disabled recovers, he resumes all of his powers. Fellman does not believe Congress, the vice president, or the cabinet should determine whether the president is unable to carry out his duties, because they would be biased. Instead, he suggests there should be a small, continuing committee that includes a member of the president's family, a justice of the Supreme Court, and ranking members of Congress from the president's own party; he does not think members of the opposing party should be put in the position of having to decide. The vice president should become acting president, not president, unless the president's disability is permanent. Fellman holds that no constitutional amendment would be necessary for this system to be established by law.

I do not know what the authors of the Constitution intended by the term 'inability,' except that they obviously intended to have the Vice President serve as Acting President during a period of Presidential disability. Disability was never defined, and was mentioned only once in the debates of the Constitutional Convention.

David Fellman, "Is a Constitutional Amendment to Provide for Cases of Presidential Disability Needed? CON," *Congressional Digest*, vol. 31, January 1958, pp. 25–30. Copyright renewed 1985 by Congressional Digest Corp. Reproduced by permission.

I think it would be extremely unwise to try to define the term 'inability' in legislation. Any attempted definition would, I believe, do more harm than good, and the more prolix [wordy] the definition, the worse it would be. Any attempt to spell out just what is meant by disability would either be tautological, repetitious, or misleading, and in any event, a sure basis for unnecessary disputation. But the law is full of undefined and undefinable terms, e.g., 'reasonable man,' 'due process of law,' 'right and equity,' etc. But certainly commonsense dictates that disability may be due either to bodily or mental infirmity, and if there is any possible doubt about it, then the law should say as much. It is certainly common knowledge that mental disability occurs, and that it can be as crippling as physical disability. If a special group or committee is created to make a finding of disability, the law should provide that (1) the finding should be in writing; (2) the finding should be based on evidence; (3) the evidence should include the testimony of physicians.

Clearly the Constitution contemplates that the President may get over his disability, since it uses the phrase 'until the disability is removed.' Obviously a sick man may get well, and the law should be clear on this point, that the President resumes all of his powers when his disability is ended.

Neither Congress nor Cabinet

I think any member of the group or committee which would be authorized by law to determine the question of the President's inability to discharge the powers and duties of his office should be eligible to initiate the question. I do not believe Congress should undertake to perform this function, mainly because the question may arise suddenly when Congress is not in session. Nor do I believe that such a numerous assemblage of men and women is equipped to make a specific decision bearing upon the qualifications of a single person upon the basis of evidence. I should think it highly improper to entrust the Vice President with the initiative, since his personal stake in the decision precludes general confidence in the objectivity of any affirmative step he may take. Since the Cabinet is made up of personal appointees of the President who serve at his pleasure, I would regard the Cabinet as wholly unsuitable to make a decision of the sort under discussion. So far as the Cabinet is concerned, the cards are stacked so heavily in favor of one disposition of the issue and against the other that an objective answer based entirely upon pertinent evidence cannot be expected in all cases.

I think Congress ought to provide for a procedure to deal with the problem of Presidential inability. For the reasons given above, the decision should not, in my judgment, be entrusted to Congress, or the Vice President, or the Cabinet. I suggest the creation by statute of a special continuing committee which would be empowered to make the critical decision of inability. While I have not given a great deal of thought to the matter of the makeup of the committee, and further reflection might suggest a somewhat different composition, I would tentatively suggest, as a basis for further discussion as follows:

1. The committee should be very small, so that it can act expeditiously and decisively. I suggest a committee of five.

2. The members of the committee could very well be the following:

(a) The President's spouse, or if there is none, the next of kin, providing he or she is an adult. (b) The Chief Justice of the United States. (c) The senior Associate Justice of the Supreme Court of the United States. (d) The leader of the President's political party in the Senate. (e) The leader of the President's political party in the House of Representatives.

Thus, such a committee would include a member of the President's family, 2 life-tenure Justices holding positions of great prestige and public confidence, and 2 ranking Members of the Houses of Congress. I would insist that members of the political party in opposition to the President should not be put in the position of participating in the decision that the President is unable to discharge the duties of his office. I think there will be greater public confidence in the participation of two important members of the President's own party.... Our President is always a partisan, and it is right that he should be a party man, since our governmental system rests upon the foundation of the party system. It is therefore altogether proper that leaders of his own party should share directly in the responsibility of making a decision of Presidential inability. Leaders of the opposition party would necessarily act under a heavy cloud of suspicion about their motives if they had a hand in the matter, however much their opinions are grounded in objective, weighty, and reliable evidence.

Such a Law Would Be Constitutional

I think a statute of the sort I have discussed is perfectly constitutional. An act of Congress seems to be fully justified by the language and purposes of article II, section 1, clause 6, of the United States Constitution.

As I have indicated, I believe that the same body ought to have authority both to initiate the question and determine its merits. I see no reason for setting up any ponderous or complex machinery. On the contrary, there is every good reason to keep the procedure uncomplicated, so that a small group of responsible people commanding public confidence can move swiftly and decisively. It might be wise to authorize the Chief Justice to take the initiative of setting the machinery in motion, but I do not see why any one of the five important people who would serve on the committee could not request a meeting of the committee for the purpose of making a decision. For example, under some circumstances the President's wife may very well be the most suitable person available to raise the question of inability. I am sure that no one of the five persons I have in mind for service on this committee would initiate action irresponsibly, partly from the very nature of their positions, and partly because the public would not stand for irresponsibility, in this connection.

The committee should be free to declare that the President is permanently disabled, if the facts warrant such a finding. Certainly it is common knowledge that there is such a thing as permanent disability. And there is no reason to believe that a committee constituted as I have suggested would make a finding of permanent disability if it were at all possible to avoid doing so. If the disability is temporary, the committee should be authorized, by the same procedure utilized to make a finding of disability, to make a finding that the President is sufficiently well to resume his duties and functions.

If the disability is temporary, I think, as I have indicated, that any member of the committee should be authorized to raise the question that the disability has ceased to exist. Once the question has been raised, it should be determined by a majority vote of the committee. As in the case of findings of disability, a finding that the disability has ended should be made in writing, on the basis of evidence, including the evidence of physicians.

Vice President as Acting President

The question whether, in the event of a finding of temporary disability, the Vice President would succeed to the powers and duties of the office, or to the office itself, is in my judgment the critical question. For there is a wide gulf between what I think was the plain intention of the framers of the Constitution and actual practice in the several instances when Vice Presidents took over upon the death of a President.

All pertinent clauses in the Constitution are consistent with the language of article II, section 1, clause 6. The 12th amendment, taking note of the fact that it might happen that neither the electoral college nor the House of Representatives may succeed in electing a new President in time, provides that 'the Vice President shall act as President, as in the case of the death or other constitutional disability of the President.' Article I, section 3, clause 5, of the Constitution provides that the Senate shall elect a President pro tempore who shall preside in the absence of the Vice President, 'or when he shall exercise the Office of President of the United States.' Note that it does not say, 'when he shall have become President,' which would have been very easy to say, if such had been the intention of those who wrote the Constitution.

The language of the Constitution, that the Vice President succeeds to the powers and duties of the President, or acts as President, or exercises the office of President, supports the view that it was not intended that he should become President. Furthermore, this is consistent with the requirements of a situation where the President's disability is only temporary. Obviously it makes more sense to say that for the duration of such a disability the Vice President shall act as President, than to say that for this period of time he shall be President, for in the latter event we would have two Presidents at the same time, which is ridiculous. But it makes sense if, while the President is too sick to discharge his duties, we have an Acting President in the person of the Vice President. Of course no such problem is posed if the President dies, or resigns, or is removed from office by impeachment, for in such cases he ceases to be President at all, and no difficulty arises if the succeeding Vice President becomes President. The real harm has been that because he is now regarded as becoming President, a solution of the problem posed by temporary Presidential disability has been frustrated.

Temporary vs. Permanent Disability

Custom has established the proposition that when a President dies the Vice President becomes President. But since we have no custom dealing with a situation created by the temporary disability of the President, I think it is altogether reasonable if a distinction is made by legislation between the two situations. We can continue on the assumption that in case the President dies, the Vice President becomes President, while at the same time we provide that in case of a temporary disability he shall serve only as Acting President, and that upon his recovery the President will reassume the powers and duties of his office. Legislation to this effect would be clearly consistent with the language and intent of article II, section 1, clause 6. As Acting President the Vice President would have all the powers of the office, such as the veto and appointive powers, but he would have to relinquish these powers upon the recovery of the President.

If a finding of permanent disability is made, I should think the Vice President would succeed to the office itself, and not merely to its powers and duties, just as he succeeds to the office if the President dies, as is now decreed by our 'unwritten Constitution.' It may of course be assumed that the committee which is authorized to make findings of disability will in the nature of things be extremely reluctant to make a finding of permanent disability, and that so long as any ray of hope exists the country would expect that the disability be regarded as temporary, if it is at all possible so to designate it. However, there is such a condition as permanent disability, and in that event I would think the existing constitutional custom would control. There does not seem to be any very good reason why it should not.

In the event of a finding of permanent disability, I believe the language of the Constitution, 'or a President shall be elected,' does not require but only authorizes the immediate election of a new President. If there should be a special election, I should think that it would be merely for the unexpired term of the disabled President, for otherwise, the sequence of events upon which the Constitution operates would be disturbed.

I believe that Congress has authority to enact legislation on all the questions raised here under the Constitution as it now stands, and that constitutional amendments are not necessary. Such legislation, based upon the language and purposes of the relevant constitutional clauses, would be justified by normal canons of constitutional construction.

A Constitutional Amendment Is Needed to Clarify the Vice President's Status in Case of Presidential Disability

George Cochran Doub

George Cochran Doub was assistant attorney general in the Civil Division of the U.S. Department of Justice. The following viewpoint is from a speech he gave in 1959 to the Federal Bar Association. In it he describes the problems that occurred when past presidents were too ill to perform their duties, and he states that such problems would endanger the nation's safety in the age of nuclear weaponry. He points out that the Constitution is not clear as to whether the vice president actually becomes president if the president cannot act, or whether he merely takes over the power and duties of the presidency. Doub writes that it is now established practice that the vice president becomes president if the incumbent president dies, but it is still unclear what happens if the president is disabled. In Doub's opinion, a constitutional amendment is needed to clarify this issue.

On March 4, 1881, James A. Garfield, who as a boy drove the mule team of a canal boat on the Ohio Canal, became President of the United States. Only four months later, Garfield drove in his carriage from the White House down Pennsylvania Avenue to the Baltimore and Potomac Railroad depot on Sixth Street intending to take a train to New England. As he walked through the station arm-in-arm with Secretary of State James G. Blaine, an assassin stepped forward with a cocked revolver and fired two shots at Garfield, striking him in the arm and side. When the lunatic, Charles J. Guiteau,

George Cochran Doub, "Presidential Disability," *Vital Speeches of the Day*, September 1, 1959.

was seized and dragged through the crowd, he cried, "Arthur is President of the United States now."

Garfield lay in a coma for 80 days completely unable to perform the duties of President. During that period, he performed only one official act—the signing of an extradition paper. The total incapacity of the President during this period, we are told, had a harmful effect on the country. Considerable Government business could not be conducted nor could important officials be appointed. It has been said that the nation's foreign relations, lacking the direction of the Chief Executive, seriously deteriorated. Only routine business was handled by Department heads.

Yet, nothing was done. There was criticism that Secretary of State Blaine was attempting to usurp the President's duties and there were insistent demands that Vice President Chester A. Arthur act. After 60 days, a Cabinet meeting was held in which it was unanimously voted that Vice President Arthur should assume the powers of the presidential office. But would he become President and thus preclude Garfield from returning to office? Opinions were divided. The members of the Cabinet voted 4-3, with Attorney General Wayne MacVeagh among the majority, that Arthur would become President and would thus permanently oust Garfield from office. The majority relied upon the fact that upon the three prior occasions of the death of the Chief Executive, the Vice President had become President and the language of the Constitution concerning death and inability was exactly the same.

The Cabinet resolved that, before Arthur should take this momentous step, Garfield should be consulted about the serious consequence to him which might attend Arthur's assumption of the powers of President. However, this could not be done by reason of Garfield's desperate condition. Arthur himself emphatically declined to take any steps to assume the powers of the President on the ground that he would not be a party to ousting Garfield from office. If Vice President Arthur had believed that he would exercise the powers of the presidency only for the duration of the President's disability, there would have been no reason for his failure to exercise those powers. Considerable sentiment developed at the time for clarification of the law, but after Garfield's death Arthur took office as President and the matter dropped.

Clarifying the Questions

If such uncertainty could occur during the peaceful days of 1881, how frightening would be the prospect of similar uncertainty at a time when it is essential that the nation have such continuity of official leadership as to enable critical decisions to be met and made.

In periods of peace and quiet of the past, this issue may not have been of vital importance but in the dangerous critical days of world leadership, of nuclear weapons, of the touch of the ICBM [intercontinental ballistic missile] on the nerve of danger, of a powerful threatening enemy, the problem becomes one of paramount consequence. In times of almost continuous international crisis requiring immediate decisions by the Executive to safeguard the nation's interests, our future safety could possibly depend upon our ability to have provided clear definitive answers to this Constitutional question.

In the event of the inability of the President to discharge the powers and duties of his office, does the Vice President succeed permanently to the Presidency? Or does he act as a temporary pinchhitter during the disability period? Who is authorized to say a President is unable to discharge his duties?

You will recall that Paragraph 6 of Section 1 of Article 2 of the Constitution provides that "in case of the removal, death, resignation and inability to discharge the powers and duties of the office of President, the same *shall* devolve on the Vice President." You will notice that the language is mandatory. "The same *shall*," not "*may*," devolve on the Vice President. "Devolve" means to pass down, descend, to transfer, and the

47

mandatory transfer to the Vice President occurs in the same way in each of the four situations: removal, death, resignation, or inability to discharge the powers and duties of the office of President. No distinction is made as to what happens in case of presidential inability and the President's removal, death, or resignation.

The Constitution states, "the same shall devolve on the Vice President." To what do the words "the same" refer? What is it that shall "devolve" upon the Vice President? Is it the *office* of the President? In that case, the President would thenceforth be permanently excluded from his office; or do only the *powers and duties* devolve upon the Vice President and in that case, his tenure as the acting chief executive would end upon the recovery of the President?

Established Practice

It appears that there was a constitutional question when the issue first arose whether the Vice President, in the case of the death of the President, became President or acting President for the balance of the term, but this doubt has now been settled by established practice.

The question first was presented when President William Henry Harrison died of pneumonia in office in 1841, one month after his inauguration. . . . Did Vice President John Tyler become President or acting President? Many objected at the time to Tyler becoming President because it was believed that the precedent would establish that the same result must occur when the President became disabled. It was argued that the records of the Constitutional Convention indicated that the Convention had not intended that the Vice President become President under the succession clause but merely that he should exercise the powers and duties of the disabled President until his disability was removed. Daniel Webster, then Secretary of State, was the only Whig who was not greatly alarmed over what the Democrat, Tyler, would do in opposition to Whig policies and interests. Webster took the position that Vice President Tyler actually became President. It was Tyler's initial belief that he would act as President during Harrison's unexpired term, but reflection changed his attitude and in his "inaugural address" he boldly proclaimed that he had been called to "the high office of this Confederacy."

The first paper submitted to Tyler for his signature had below the space for his signature the words "Acting President." Tyler was incensed and by a stroke of his pen eliminated the word "Acting" and signed as President, and President he became. After him, six other Vice Presidents, Fillmore, Johnson, Arthur, Theodore Roosevelt, Coolidge and Truman, did likewise upon the death of the President in office. From these precedents, it is now assumed that, in the case of the death of a President, the Vice President becomes President for the unexpired term. Yet, the very way the original doubt was resolved by these precedents has contributed to the problem in the case of the inability of the President to discharge the powers and duties of his office.

When we examine the original articles agreed upon in substance by the Constitutional Convention before their revision by the Committee of Style, we find that they made clear that upon the inability of the President to discharge the powers and duties of his office, the Vice President should exercise those powers and duties "until the inability of the President be removed."

In other words, the framers of the Constitution intended that the Vice President would be acting as President, but would not become the President. Although acting as President, he would remain in the office of Vice President.

The obscurity developed by reason of the revision made by the Committee of Style, which boiled the provision down to the simplified statement that in case of removal, death, resignation or inability to discharge the powers and duties of the office, "the same shall devolve on the Vice President."

This interpretation is borne out by the debates in the Convention indicating that the Vice Presidency was originally created to provide for an alternate chief executive who might function from time to time should the President be unable to exercise the powers and duties of his office. Indeed, only after the Convention decided upon this standby position did the Convention consider giving the Vice President something to do while he waited in the wings. The idea of assigning him the duty of presiding over the Senate seems to have been an afterthought.

Woodrow Wilson's Illness

In 1919, President Woodrow Wilson suffered a stroke while leading his great fight for the adoption of the Covenant of the League of Nations. . . .

The illness of Wilson continued from his collapse on September 25, 1919, until the end of his presidential term on March 4, 1921. During this period of one year and five months, the President was unable to attend any Cabinet meetings or to perform most of his duties. The exact extent of his inability is not clear because his condition was carefully shielded from the public by Mrs. Wilson, his personal physician and his entourage in the White House. Indeed, even the Vice President and the Cabinet were kept in the dark about Wilson's condition. It is said that for a considerable period of time—although the precise time is subject to speculation—he was completely unable to perform *any* of the duties of his high office. It has been believed that Mrs. Wilson and the President's physician played a major role in making and deciding matters of large public policy. In any event, the administration of the Government almost was at a standstill for one and a half years. . . .

Now why did Wilson's personal advisers fear knowledge of his disability becoming known? I believe that there can be no doubt that a primary reason was because of their fear that public opinion would demand that Vice President Marshall take over the powers of the Presidency and, if Wilson should recover, he might face a constitutional fight to regain his office. In other words, the dangerous uncertainty of this constitutional provision was responsible for this deplorable situation. . . .

The pernicious consequences of the belief that a vice president actually succeeds to the presidency for the balance of the presidential term, when called upon to exercise the powers and duties of a disabled president, have been in both the Garfield and the Wilson case to frustrate the intent of the drafters of the Constitution that the nation should have an alternate chief executive ready to provide continuous executive leadership. . . .

Eisenhower's Plan

Immediately upon President [Dwight] Eisenhower's recovery from his heart attack in Colorado in September, 1955, he directed the Department of Justice to institute a full legal study of the constitutional problem with respect to presidential inability. . . .

President Eisenhower was the first President of the United States who had the courage, the interest and the appreciation of the problem to attempt to correct this serious deficiency of the Constitution. Every prior president shrank from attempting to deal with this delicate matter or manifested no realization of the difficulty.

On March 3, 1958, the President and the Vice President took an historic step in consultation with Attorney General William P. Rogers when they reduced to memorandum form, and published, their own understanding of the constitutional role of the Vice President as acting President during the disability of the President. The Eisenhower-Nixon understanding was stated in these terms:

The President and the Vice President have agreed that the following procedures are in accord with the purposes and provisions of Article 2, Section 1, of the Constitution, dealing with Presidential inability. They believe that these procedures, which are intended to apply to themselves only, are in no sense outside or contrary to the Constitution but are consistent with its present provisions and implement its clear intent.

1. In the event of inability the President would—if possible—so inform the Vice President, and the Vice President, would serve as Acting President, exercising the powers and duties of the office until the inability had ended.

2. In the event of an inability which would prevent the President from communicating with the Vice President, the Vice President, after such consultation as seems to him appropriate under the circumstances, would decide upon the devolution of the powers and duties of the Office and would serve as Acting President until the inability had ended.

3. The President, in either event, would determine when the inability had ended and at that time would resume the full exercise of the powers and duties of the Office.

I have no doubt that this unprecedented document, although not binding upon future Presidents and Vice Presidents, will become recognized as a notable State Paper of our Constitutional history.

A Proposed Amendment

On the day following the Eisenhower-Nixon announcement a bipartisan majority of the members of the Senate Judiciary Committee ... joined in sponsoring a proposed constitutional amendment on presidential inability which adopted the Administration's proposal with certain changes in Section 4 acceptable to the Executive. This proposed bipartisan amendment was promptly introduced in the Congress.

Section 1 restates existing law in case of the removal, death or resignation of the President.

Section 2 provides that, if a President declares in writing that he is unable to discharge the powers and duties of his office, those powers and duties shall be discharged by the Vice President as acting President. This section assures a President in announcing his own inability that his powers and duties will be restored to him upon his recovery.

Section 3 deals with a situation in which the President is unable or unwilling to declare his own disability. In that case, the Vice President with the approval of the majority of the heads of the Executive Departments in office—that is to say, the President's Cabinet—shall make this decision. Many scholars agree that the Vice President alone now has the authority under the Constitution to make this determination. Section 3 requires the written concurrence of a majority of the members of the Cabinet.

Section 4 provides that, whenever the President declares in writing that his disability is terminated, he shall resume the exercise of the powers and duties of his office. This provision affords a constitutional guarantee to a President that he will regain the powers of his office when his disability has been removed.

The realities of the situation suggest that it is unlikely a Vice President would attempt to assume the duties of the Presidency unless it were clear beyond challenge that the President was in fact unable to exercise the responsibilities of the office. . . .

Historically this problem has never been one of a too aggressive Vice President but rather of a reluctant Vice President, who hesitated to exercise the powers of the President under the present succession clause of the Constitution because of the uncertainty that his action might result in the permanent elimination of the President from his office.

The essential solution is a clarifying amendment establishing that the Vice President's tenure of the presidential powers is only temporary. This provision is the foundation of the administration's proposal submitted in 1957, resubmitted in 1958, and the bipartisan amendment proposed in the same year. The proposal implements the original understanding of the members of the Constitutional Convention as indicated in the debates and in the original articles.

There is now presented the best opportunity in our history for the solution of this problem. The time required for the ratification of a constitutional amendment will undoubtedly extend beyond the term of this administration and accordingly will be inapplicable to it. We do not know the person or the party that will occupy the White House in 1961, but we do know that under the Constitution, it will not be President Eisenhower. At this moment in history, the proposed measure can be considered entirely upon its merits without any consideration of personalities or parties.

The Nation Must Not Be Left Without a Vice President

Richard M. Nixon

Richard M. Nixon was the thirty-seventh president of the United States, serving from 1969 to 1974. Earlier, between 1953 and 1961, he was vice president under Dwight Eisenhower. He wrote the following article shortly after the 1963 assassination of President John F. Kennedy. In it he points out that during the nation's history the office of vice president has frequently been empty, and that the law determining succession to the presidency when there is no vice president has been changed several times. The responsibilities of the vice president have grown, he says, and should not be given to the Speaker of the House, who already holds a burdensome office and who may be of a different party than the president. There have been several proposals to solve this problem, Nixon says. In his opinion they are not feasible, and the best solution would be a constitutional amendment giving the Electoral College power to elect a new vice president. But whatever is done, he argues, Congress needs to act quickly, and it is essential to remember that the vice president must have the ability and experience to lead the nation in perilous times.

The eight weeks that have passed since the assassination of President [John F.] Kennedy have been a period of great soul searching for the American people. We have asked ourselves how this tragic act of violence could have happened in our country. We have urged that steps be taken to provide better protection for our Presidents in the future.

We have also taken a new, hard look at the question of presidential succession. And we have concluded that there is a serious deficiency in an otherwise remarkable constitutional process.

Richard M. Nixon, "We Need a Vice President Now," *Saturday Evening Post*, January 18, 1964, pp. 6–10. Copyright © 1964 Saturday Evening Post Society. Reproduced by permission.

In the event of a vacant vice presidential office, President Richard Nixon advocated the establishment of a Constitutional amendment that permits the election of a new vice president to the Electoral College. The Library of Congress.

While everyone knows that eight Vice Presidents have succeeded to the presidency upon the death of an incumbent, it is not so well known that another seven Vice Presidents of the United States have died in office, and one has even resigned.

The Office of the Vice President has been vacant 16 times. In other words, during over 40 years of our history, this nation has not had a Vice President and there has been no constitutionally elected successor to the President.

Three times the Congress has dealt with this problem.

The first law, passed in 1792, made the President *pro tempore* [for the time being] of the Senate and then the Speaker of the House of Representatives the next in the line of presidential succession after the Vice President. These congressional officers were put ahead of the President's Cabinet because [Alexander] Hamilton, the Federalist Party leader, wished to block the path of Secretary of State [Thomas] Jefferson.

This law was changed in 1886, during the Democratic Administration of Grover Cleveland. His Vice President had died the year before, and the Senate was controlled by the Republicans. To prevent the possible elevation of a member of the opposition party to the White House, the line of succession was given to the Cabinet, starting with the Secretary of State.

The last change was proposed by President [Harry S.] Truman in 1945. He requested Congress to make the Speaker of the House his successor. Some observers at the time suggested that he was motivated by the belief that Speaker [Sam] Rayburn would make a better President than Secretary of State [Edward] Stettinius. And so, since 1947, when this law was enacted, the line of succession to the presidency has run: Vice President, Speaker of the House of Representatives, President *pro tempore* of the Senate, the Secretary of State, and finally the other members of the Cabinet.

A New Law Is Needed

Assuming that a law should be written for all time and not just to deal with a temporary situation, the conclusion is inescapable that the laws of presidential succession have in the past been enacted for the wrong reasons.

Now is the time to make a change for the *right* reason.

The right reason is not that a Speaker of the House is always less qualified to be President than a Secretary of State. Sam Rayburn, for example, would have been a better President than Edward Stettinius. And the present Speaker, John W. McCormack, is a man with a distinguished record of 40 years' service to our nation, who has always stood in the forefront of the fight against Communism both at home and abroad.

Yet as recent Presidents have rightly given more and more responsibilities to their Vice Presidents, the present system now raises to what has truly become the second office in the land a man who already holds one of the most burdensome offices of government—the Speaker of the House. Moreover, it is not unlikely that a Speaker could be of a different party from the President's. This was the case during the 80th Congress when President Truman would have been succeeded by Republican Speaker Joseph Martin.

So, putting present personalities aside, we must write a new law of presidential succession. And as did the framers of our Constitution, we must write for posterity, not merely for the moment.

There have been three serious proposals recently made for changing the law of presidential succession.

First. It has been proposed that we go back to the old system of putting the Secretary of State and the Cabinet ahead of the Speaker of the House in the line of succession. But a good Secretary of State doesn't necessarily make a good President. While a particular Secretary of State might be an excellent choice, just as a particular Speaker might be, this proposal offers us no such guarantee. It is significant to note that no one who has held the office of Secretary of State has been elected to the presidency since James Buchanan. And, as President Truman suggested in 1945, I believe there are advantages in elevating a man to the presidency through the elective, rather than the appointive, office.

Second. It has been proposed that the Congress elect a new Vice President. A similar plan would have the President appoint a Vice President with the consent of the Congress. Both of these proposals, however, could create grave difficulties if the Congress happened to be controlled by the opposition party, which has been the case during the terms of 16 Presidents.

Third. Senator Kenneth Keating of New York has introduced a constitutional amendment to provide for the election of two Vice Presidents. First in the line of succession would be an Executive Vice President who would have no other constitutional duties. The second Vice President, or Legislative Vice President, would then follow in the line of succession, and would have the constitutional duties of presiding over the Senate and breaking tie votes. The major disadvantage of this novel proposal is that by dividing the already limited functions of the office, we would be downgrading the vice presidency at a time when it is imperative that we add to its prestige and importance.

How can we best design a new law which will not have these objections? I believe the trouble in the past was that changes in the law of succession have been made to deal with an immediate, personal situation. Because it was thought that a particular individual should not be President, the plan was changed to block that man. Instead of trying to devise a plan which will promote or block a particular man, what we need to do is to direct our thoughts generally to the question of the kind of man who would be best fitted to succeed to the presidency of the United States and then design a plan which will find that man.

Vice Presidential Qualifications

What qualifications should a Vice President have?

He should be a man qualified to be President.

He should be a full-time Vice President with no other official duties.

He should be a member of the same political party as the President.

He should have a political philosophy which is close to that of the President, particularly in the field of foreign affairs.

He should be personally acceptable to the President, but since he may potentially hold the highest office in the land, his selection should reflect the elective, rather than the appointive, process.

What kind of plan will allow the selection of such a man?

The Electoral College Proposal

I believe there is one proposal that has not been given adequate consideration to date and that would best accomplish this purpose. It would take the form of an amendment to Article II, Section I, of the Constitution and would read as follows:

> Within thirty days after a vacancy occurs in the Office of Vice President, either because of death, removal, or the elevation of the incumbent to the presidency, the President shall reconvene the Electoral College for the purpose of electing a Vice President of the United States.

This proposal, as is the case with Senator Keating's, recognizes that merely changing the law of succession does not necessarily fill the Office of the Vice President. And the Office of Vice President itself, apart from the question of succession, has become necessary to the country.

By using the Electoral College as the instrument for selecting a new Vice President, we would be relying on a popularly elected constitutional body which in contrast to the Congress always reflects the will of the people as of the last presidential election. While it is true that the Electoral College is now a constitutional anachronism, this important new function would upgrade the body and would bring about the selection of more responsible persons to serve on it.

Besides filling the vice presidency and reflecting the will of the electorate, this plan assures continuity of programs and the selection of a Vice President who can work with the President. For, as in the case of the nominating conventions, where the presidential candidate has the greatest voice in selecting his running mate, so too could we expect the President to have the greatest influence in the deliberations of the Electoral College. He would probably recommend the man most acceptable to him as the new Vice President.

But the fact that the Electoral College would have the final authority to make the decision would be a safeguard against arbitrary action on his part. Most important, it would mean that whoever held the Office of President or Vice President would always be a man selected by the people directly or by their elected representatives, rather than a man who gained the office by appointment.

Congress Must Act

We now come to the most critical question of all—how do we get action on this or one of the other proposals which have been made to deal with the problem of presidential succession?

The failure of the Congress to act on the equally important question of presidential disability is a case in point. The Constitution does not set forth a procedure as to how and when the Vice President shall assume the duties of President when the President is unable to serve because of illness. Fifty years ago the country could afford to "muddle along" until the disabled President either got well or died. But today when only the President can make the decision to use atomic weapons in the defense of the nation, there could be a critical period when "no finger is on the trigger" because of the illness of the Chief Executive.

After his heart attack in 1955, President [Dwight D.] Eisenhower asked the Congress to correct this situation. When the Congress failed to act, he took matters in his own hands and in 1958 wrote me a letter the key paragraphs of which follow:

The President and the Vice President have agreed that the following procedures are in accord with the purposes and provisions of Article 2, Section 1, of the Constitution, dealing with presidential inability. They believe that these procedures, which are intended to apply to themselves only, are in no sense outside or contrary to the Constitution but are consistent with its present provisions and implement its clear intent.

1. In the event of inability a President would—if possible—so inform the Vice President, and the Vice President would serve as acting President, exercising the powers and duties of the office until the inability had ended.

2. In the event of an inability which would prevent the President from so communicating with the Vice President, the Vice President, after such consultation as seems to him appropriate under the circumstances, would decide upon the devolution of the powers and duties of the Office and would serve as Acting President until the inability had ended.

3. The President, in either event, would determine when the inability had ended and at that time would resume the full exercise of the powers and duties of the Office.

This historic document was later adopted by President Kennedy, and most recently by President [Lyndon B.] Johnson. But it must be remembered that this procedure is merely a stopgap. It does not have the force of law. I strongly believe that either legislation or a constitutional amendment should be enacted to solve this problem on a permanent basis.

The time has come to give top priority to the consideration of proposals to deal with both presidential succession and presidential disability. The most effective way to get action is to set up a bipartisan Presidential Commission, such as the famed Hoover Commission on the Reorganization of the Executive Branch of Government. President Johnson might appoint to the commission to serve as public members our three former Presidents, [Herbert] Hoover, Truman and Eisenhower. The Speaker and the President *pro tempore* of the Senate would appoint the six other members from the House and Senate. The recommendations of such a distinguished, blue-ribbon panel would not only be of great merit, they would, with the backing of the President, be almost sure to become the law of the land.

A Defect in the Constitutional Process

It is a tragic fact that it took a terrible crime in Dallas to remind us of a serious defect in our constitutional process. The murder of our President has forced us to reassess our law of succession and the Office of the Vice President.

Both Presidents Eisenhower and Kennedy recognized the importance of the vice presidency as no other Presidents had done before them. The extensive duties assigned to Vice President Johnson and myself, at home and abroad, were unprecedented in our history. The country now feels safer and more confident because of the experience that Mr. Johnson gained while serving under President Kennedy. Clearly there can be no reversal of this trend toward greater duties and responsibilities for the Vice President.

When a President dies in office, the man in his party who has been best trained for the presidency should succeed him. The vice presidency today, as a result of the way both President Eisenhower and President Kennedy upgraded the position, is the only office which provides complete on-the-job training for the duties of the presidency.

We have swiftly and dramatically been reminded again that when we choose a man for Vice President we may also be choosing a man who will become President. This means that our presidential nominating conventions can no longer fall back on the politically cynical formulas of "balancing the ticket"—of choosing a Westerner for Vice President only because the presidential candidate is an Easterner, or a conservative because the standard-bearer is a liberal.

From now on it is absolutely essential that both political-party conventions nominate two Presidents—candidates for both national offices, President *and* Vice President—who have the ability and experience to lead the United States of America in these perilous times.

Congress Should Act to Amend the Constitution Regarding Executive Succession

Lyndon B. Johnson

Lyndon B. Johnson was the thirty-sixth president of the United States, serving from 1963 to 1969. As vice president, he succeeded to the presidency on the death of President John F. Kennedy. For a time, no vice president was serving under him, and he was well aware of the potential problem this caused. The following viewpoint is a message he sent to Congress in 1965 urging legislators to act on a constitutional amendment to deal with cases of presidential disability and with vacancies in the office of vice president. He also proposes reforms in the Electoral College system. A nation bearing responsibilities not only for its own security but also for the security of the free world cannot justify, he says, the gamble of entrusting leadership to a commander in chief who is unable to command.

In 1787, Benjamin Franklin remarked near the conclusion of the Constitutional Convention at Philadelphia, "It . . . astonishes me, Sir, to find this system approaching so near to perfection as it does. . . ."

One-hundred-seventy-eight years later the relevance of that Constitution of 1789 to our society of 1965 is remarkable. Yet it is truly astonishing that, over this span, we have neither perfected the provisions for orderly continuity in the Executive direction of our system nor, as yet, paid the price our continuing inaction so clearly invites and so recklessly risks.

Lyndon B. Johnson, "Special Message to Congress on Presidential Disability and Related Matters," The American Presidency Project, January 28, 1965. © 1999–2009—Gerhard Peters—The American Presidency Project. Reproduced by permission.

I refer, of course, to three conspicuous and long-recognized defects in the Constitution relating to the Office of the Presidency:

1. The lack of a constitutional provision assuring the orderly discharge of the powers and duties of the President—Commander-in-Chief—in the event of the disability or incapacity of the incumbent.

2. The lack of a constitutional provision assuring continuity in the Office of the Vice President, an Office which itself is provided within our system for the primary purpose of assuring continuity.

3. The lack of a constitutional provision assuring that the votes of electors in the Electoral College shall without question reflect the expressed will of the people in the actual election of their President and Vice President.

Chasms of Chaos

Over the years, as I have noted, we have escaped the mischief these obvious omissions invite and permit. Our escape has been more the result of Providence than of any prudence on our part. For it is not necessary to conjure the nightmare of nuclear holocaust or other national catastrophe to identify these omissions as chasms of chaos into which normal human frailties might plunge us at any time.

On at least two occasions in our history, and perhaps others, American presidents—James Garfield and Woodrow Wilson—have for prolonged periods been rendered incapable of discharging their Presidential duties. On sixteen occasions in our thirty-six Administrations, the Office of Vice President has been vacant—and over the two perilous decades since the end of the Second World War, that vital office has been vacant the equivalent of one year out of four. Finally, over recent years, complex but concerted campaigns have been openly undertaken—fortunately without success, as yet—to subvert the

Electoral College so that it would register not the will of the people of individual states but, rather, the wishes of the electors themselves.

The potential of paralysis implicit in these conditions constitutes an indefensible folly for our responsible society in these times. Common sense impels, duty requires us to act—and to act now, without further delay.

Action is in the tradition of our forebears. Since adoption of "The Bill of Rights"—the first ten Amendments to our Constitution—nine of the fourteen subsequent Amendments have related directly either to the Offices of the Presidency and Vice Presidency or to assuring the responsiveness of our voting processes to the will of the people. As long ago as 1804 and as recently as 1964, Americans have amended their Constitution in striving for its greater perfection in these most sensitive and critical areas.

I believe it is the strong and overriding will of the people today that we should act now to eliminate these unhappy possibilities inherent in our system as it now exists. Likewise, I believe it is the consensus of an overwhelming majority of the Congress—without thought of partisanship—that effective action be taken promptly. I am, accordingly, addressing this communication to both Houses to ask that this prevailing will be translated into action which would permit the people, through the process of constitutional amendment, to overcome these omissions so clearly evident in our system.

The Nation Must Be Prepared

I. *Presidential Inability* Our Constitution clearly prescribes the order of procedure for assuring continuity in the Office of the Presidency in the event of the death of the incumbent. These provisions have met their tragic tests successfully. Our system, unlike many others, has never experienced the catastrophe of disputed succession or the chaos of uncertain command.

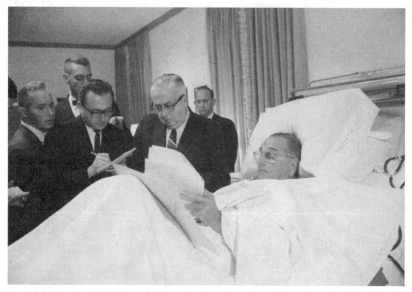

President Lyndon B. Johnson looks over documents in his hospital bed. After John F. Kennedy's death, Johnson succeeded to the presidency, leaving the office of vice president vacant for a time. © Betmann/Corbis.

Our stability is, nonetheless, more superficial than sure. While we are prepared for the possibility of a President's death, we are all but defenseless against the probability of a President's incapacity by injury, illness, senility or other affliction. A nation bearing the responsibilities we are privileged to bear for our own security—and the security of the Free World—cannot justify the appalling gamble of entrusting its security to the immobilized hands or uncomprehending mind of a Commander-in-Chief unable to command.

On September 29, 1964, the Senate passed Senate Joint Resolution 139, proposing a constitutional amendment to deal with this perplexing question of Presidential disability—as well as the question, which I shall discuss below, of filling vacancies in the Office of Vice President. The same measure has been introduced in this Congress as S.J. Res. 1 and H.J. Res. 1. The provisions of these measures have been carefully considered and are the product of many of our finest constitutional and legal minds. Believing, as I do, that S.J. Res. 1 and H.J. Res. 1 would responsibly meet the pressing need I have outlined, I urge the Congress to approve them forthwith for submission to ratification by the states.

Vice Presidential Vacancy

II. *Vacancy in the Office of the Vice President* Indelible personal experience has impressed upon me the indisputable logic and imperative necessity of assuring that the Second Office of our system shall, like the First Office, be at all times occupied by an incumbent who is able and who is ready to assume the powers and duties of the Chief Executive and Commander-in-Chief.

In our history, to this point, the Office of the Presidency has never devolved below the first clearly-prescribed step of constitutional succession. In moments of need, there has always been a Vice President, yet Vice Presidents are no less mortal than Presidents. Seven men have died in the Office and one has resigned—in addition to the eight who left the Office vacant to succeed to the Presidency.

We recognized long ago the necessity of assuring automatic succession in the absence of a Vice President. Various statutes have been enacted at various times prescribing orders of succession from among either the presiding officers of the Houses of Congress or the heads of Executive Departments who, together, comprise the traditional Cabinet of the President. In these times, such orders of succession are no substitute for an office of succession.

Since the last order of succession was prescribed by the Congress in 1947, the Office of the Vice Presidency has undergone the most significant transformation and enlargement of duties in its history.

Presidents [Harry S.] Truman, [Dwight D.] Eisenhower and [John F.] Kennedy have successively expanded the role of the Vice President, even as I expect to do in this Administration.

Once only an appendage, the Office of Vice President is an integral part of the chain of command and its occupancy on a full-time basis is imperative.

For this reason, I most strongly endorse the objective of both S.J. Res. 1 and H.J. Res. 1 in providing that whenever there is a vacancy in the Office of Vice President, provision shall exist for that Office to be filled with a person qualified to succeed to the Presidency.

Reforming the Electoral College

III. *Reform of the Electoral College System* We believe that the people should elect their President and Vice President. One of the earliest amendments to our Constitution was submitted and ratified in response to the unhappy experience of an Electoral College stalemate which jeopardized this principle. Today there lurks in the Electoral College system the ever-present possibility that electors may substitute their own will for the will of the people. I believe that possibility should be foreclosed.

Our present system of computing and awarding electoral votes by states is an essential counterpart of our Federal system and the provisions of our Constitution which recognize and maintain our nation as a union of states. It supports the two party system which has served our nation well. I believe this system should be retained. But it is imperative that the electoral votes of a state be cast for those persons who receive the greatest number of votes for President and Vice President—and for no one else.

At the same time, I believe we should eliminate the omission in our present system which leaves the continuity of the offices of President and Vice President unprotected if the persons receiving a majority of the electoral votes for either or both of these offices should die after the election in November and before the Inauguration of the President. Electors are now legally free to choose the President without regard to the outcome of the election. I believe that if the President-Elect dies under these circumstances, our laws should provide that the Vice President-Elect should become President when the new term begins. Conversely, if death should come to the Vice President-Elect during this interim, I believe the President-Elect should, upon taking office, be required to follow the procedures otherwise prescribed for filling the unexpired term of the Vice President. If both should die or become unable to serve in this interim, I believe the Congress should be made responsible for providing the method of selecting officials for both positions. I am transmitting herewith a draft Amendment to the Constitution to resolve these problems.

Favorable action by the Congress on the measures here recommended will, I believe, assure the orderly continuity in the Presidency that is imperative to the success and stability of our system. Action on these measures now will allay future anxiety among our own people—and among the peoples of the world—in the event senseless tragedy or unforeseeable disability should strike again at either or both of the principal offices of our constitutional system. If we act now, without undue delay, we shall have moved closer to achieving perfection of the great constitutional document on which the strength and success of our system have rested for nearly two centuries.

The Twenty-fifth Amendment Closes a Crucial Gap in Governmental Structure

John P. MacKenzie

John P. MacKenzie was a staff writer for The Washington Post. *In the following newspaper article, written a few days after Congress sent the Twenty-fifth Amendment to the states for ratification, he states that although the amendment will not solve every crisis that might result from the disability of a president, it goes a long way toward eliminating possible chaos. He describes the provisions of the amendment and explains what would have happened if it had been in effect at the time of several past presidential illnesses. MacKenzie projects that it will not be ratified for nearly two years but that once that happens the nation will be more secure.*

The 25th Amendment to the United States Constitution, which is on its way to the states for ratification, will not solve every crisis of executive power that springs from the disability of a President. Its strongest supporters make no such claim for it.

But the proposed Amendment goes a long way toward taking the chaos out of potential crisis. It relies on the strengths of the American political system to carry the country the rest of the way.

The Amendment closes a great gap in the governmental structure by allowing a disabled President to turn over his powers to the Vice President temporarily. But it does not tell the Chief Executive how to assess his disability or how to decide when he's ready to resume office.

No Guidelines

The Amendment outlines a procedure for a Vice President to assume the office when a President cannot or will not disqualify himself.

But there are no guidelines in the Amendment—or anywhere else in the written Constitution or laws—to tell the Vice President when that awesome political decision must be made.

In the number of political checks and balances that it provides, as well as in the wide range of political action that it lets alone, the proposed Amendment resembles the basic Constitution itself: A broadly framed document that lays down major government outlines and leaves much to the good sense of the people.

Clear on Succession

Section 1 of the Amendment makes clear that when a President dies, the Vice President succeeds to all his powers.

Section 2 says that a vacancy in the Vice Presidency must be filled by the President's nomination and confirmation by majority vote of the House and the Senate.

Section 3 allows the President, by writing to Congress that he is disabled, to turn over his powers to the Vice President as Acting President until he writes Congress that he's ready to return.

Section 4, which covers disagreement over a President's physical or mental condition, provides the most fascinating possibilities for testing the constitutional formula of broad ground rules plus good political sense.

Spells Out Procedure

Under this section if a President were prevented from declaring his own disability—for example, if he lay mortally wounded as James A. Garfield did for 80 days, or if he were kidnaped by a hostile power—the Vice President and a majority of the Cabinet could inform Congress of the disability and the Vice President automatically would become Acting President.

In case of disagreement between the President on one hand and the Vice President and Cabinet majority on the other, appeal would be made to Congress.

The Vice President would take over in the interim. Congress would have to assemble within 48 hours and would have 21 days to decide the issue. The balance here would be tipped toward the President, with two-thirds vote of each house required to keep him from resuming office.

Covers Contingencies

One other wrinkle in the Amendment allows Congress to substitute for the Cabinet another body to determine the President's condition. This covers such contingencies as the President's firing his Cabinet or the Cabinet's siding with the President in the face of overwhelming evidence of disability.

Some historical "ifs" come into play in considering how the country might have fared under the 25th Amendment during the famous disabilities of President Garfield, [Woodrow] Wilson and [Dwight D.] Eisenhower.

Garfield's Cabinet was unanimous in its view that Vice President Chester A. Arthur should assume the Presidency, but most of the Cabinet members also felt that Garfield could not have resumed office upon recovery.

Long Leaderless

The 25th Amendment, with its assurance of a procedure for restoring Garfield, might have tempered Arthur's reluctance to take over the office, and the Nation might have been leaderless for a shorter time.

If the 25th Amendment had been in force during the Wilson disability, the White House hardly could have kept the

Ratification of the 25th Amendment

State	Date Ratified	State	Date Ratified
Alabama	March 14, 1967	Montana	February 15, 1967
Alaska	February 18, 1966	Nebraska	July 12, 1965
Arizona	September 22, 1965	Nevada	February 10, 1967
Arkansas	November 4, 1965	New Hampshire	June 13, 1966
California	October 21, 1965	New Jersey	November 29, 1965
Colorado	February 3, 1966	New Mexico	February 3, 1966
Connecticut	February 14, 1967	New York	March 14, 1966
Delaware	December 7, 1965	North Carolina	March 22, 1967
Florida	May 25, 1967	North Dakota	NA
Georgia	NA	Ohio	March 7, 1967
Hawaii	March 3, 1966	Oklahoma	July 16, 1965
Idaho	March 2, 1966	Oregon	February 2, 1967
Illinois	March 22, 1967	Pennsylvania	August 18, 1965
Indiana	October 20, 1965	Rhode Island	January 28, 1966
Iowa	January 26, 1967	South Carolina	NA
Kansas	February 8, 1966	South Dakota	March 6, 1967
Kentucky	September 15, 1965	Tennessee	January 12, 1967
Louisiana	July 5, 1966	Texas	April 25, 1967
Maine	January 24, 1966	Utah	January 17, 1966
Maryland	March 23, 1966	Vermont	February 10, 1966
Massachusetts	August 9, 1965	Virginia	March 8, 1966
Michigan	October 5, 1965	Washington	January 26, 1967
Minnesota	February 10, 1967	West Virginia	January 20, 1966
Mississippi	March 10, 1966	Wisconsin	July 13, 1965
Missouri	March 30, 1966	Wyoming	January 25, 1967

TAKEN FROM: Compiled by editor.

Cabinet and Vice President Thomas R. Marshall in the dark about the President's condition. The very existence of a procedure to appeal the disability question to Congress might well have opened up the White House to the counsels of the rest of the Administration.

Possibly a constitutional provision for an Acting President would have led Wilson to relinquish the presidential powers temporarily. Perhaps such a constitutional scheme would have helped overcome Marshall's extreme reluctance to take executive action. And "iffiest" of all, the United States thus might have salvaged something from the League of Nations fight by substituting compromise for Wilson's intransigence.

Different Disabilities

Any of the three Eisenhower disabilities—the 1955 heart attack, the 1956 ileitis operation and the slight stroke he suffered in 1957—might have been handled differently. By no means would any or all of the illnesses have required a transfer of authority. But a flexible procedure would have been available to cope with a sudden world crisis, and the Nation would have been less anxious for that.

In the use of the Amendment tool, all the existing political rules would apply. Before acting, political leaders would measure the President's condition against the world situation and the state of public opinion as well as the political consequences to themselves.

The 25th Amendment would not eliminate all possibilities for intrigue or a "palace revolt." But it would spread responsibility for a change in power and would diminish the opportunity for mischief.

Indispensable Party

The Vice President would be the one indispensable party to any change and the checks against ill-considered action by the Vice President are impressive in themselves.

The Amendment's congressional pilot, Sen. Birch Bayh (D-Ind.), said Tuesday in the closing Senate debate, "In a time of national crisis, the American people would not tolerate an act on the part of the Vice President that was not in the best interests of the country."

Minority Leader Everett M. Dirksen (R-Ill.) said of the possibility of vice presidential mischiefs, "I cannot imagine it, because, after all, the people of this country will have something to say about that. Where would it lead? They would not exactly run him out on a rail, but his whole political future, such as it might be, would come to an end at that point."

A Further Safeguard

A further safeguard lies in the modern practice of selecting Vice Presidents with an eye to more than ticket-balancing. Loyalty and executive ability are increasingly recognized as essentials and Presidents would be even more careful about choosing their Cabinets as well.

Ohio's Senate ratified the Amendment [right away], before the General Services Administration had time to transmit the official papers. The Wisconsin Assembly also has acted, putting Wisconsin and Ohio in a race to be the first ratifying state.

Three fourths of the state legislatures must ratify the Amendment within seven years to make it effective. Because of the timing of state legislative sessions, the 38th state is not expected to ratify before early 1967.

But when that happens, the Nation will find itself a little less dependent on the colossal luck it has enjoyed for 187 years. And Americans will have given their system a vote of confidence.

CHAPTER 2

The Twenty-fifth
Amendment in Action

The Twenty-fifth Amendment Was First Used When Gerald Ford Became Vice President

John D. Feerick

John D. Feerick is the Norris Professor of Law at the Fordham University School of Law. In the following chapter from his book on the Twenty-fifth Amendment, he relates how it was used for the first time in 1973, when Vice President Spiro Agnew resigned while facing criminal charges of tax fraud. Before Agnew's resignation, there was considerable speculation about who would be nominated to replace him. Leaders of the Democratic Party did not want a prominent person who was likely to run against them in the next election. Also, because President Richard Nixon was involved in the Watergate scandal and might be impeached, it was known that whoever was chosen as vice president might soon succeed him. Nixon nominated Gerald Ford, the minority leader of the House of Representatives, who was not well known to the public. During the confirmation hearings held by Congress he was subjected to an exhaustive investigation. Many in Congress disagreed with his views, but some insisted that under the Twenty-fifth Amendment the president had the right to choose someone who shared his own views. In the end, Feerick notes, Ford was confirmed on the basis of his integrity.

Speculation about a new Vice President to replace [Spiro] Agnew began weeks before his resignation. In September 1973, in anticipation of Agnew's resignation, three major congressional committees began to study secretly the process by which a vice presidential vacancy would be filled. It is not surprising that, at about the same time, various names were mentioned in the press as possible replacements. . . .

John D. Feerick, *The Twenty-Fifth Amendment: Its Complete History and Application*, Bronx, NY: Fordham University Press, 1992. Copyright © 1992 by Fordham University Press. All rights reserved. Reproduced by permission.

On September 20, at a meeting with Democratic freshmen members of the House, the House Democratic leaders indicated that they would insist that the President nominate a caretaker Vice President who would pledge not to run for President in 1976. One of the leaders reportedly said: "'We're not going to be a party to picking somebody who is going to run against us three years from now.'" . . .

The idea of a caretaker Vice President was soundly denounced in the press, and an Oliver Quayle poll revealed that 93 per cent of the people were opposed to the proposal. Senator [Birch] Bayh declared that the Twenty-Fifth Amendment did not contemplate a caretaker Vice President. "'If a man happens to be in the running in 1976,'" said Bayh, "'that's just a fact of political life.'" "'From the practical standpoint,'" he added, "'we should find someone who's going to be a good Vice President and a good President.'" He concluded by saying that the consideration "'has to be out of the partisan arena.'" Governor [of Oregon Tom] McCall put it sharply: "'This idea that you can have some doddering nincompoop caretaker in there when America is on her death bed, when the President could fall in a day, is nonsense.'" . . .

A Nomination Is Made

[Gerald] Ford . . . had emerged as a favorite-son type of candidate among the members of Congress and of the Republican National Committee. Yet, declared John Herbers of *The New York Times* in its issue of October 12: "The boom for Representative Ford was considered more an expression of loyalty by his friends in the Congress than a serious effort to make him Vice President."

Without indicating his choice, President Nixon scheduled a nationwide television and radio address from the White House for October 12 at 9:00 P.M. He advised Ford of his selection as the vice presidential nominee around 7:30 P.M. Shortly after 9:00, in a brief speech from the East Room of the

White House before scores of congressional and other governmental leaders, Nixon announced his choice to the nation. He said that Ford met the criteria he had set—that he was qualified to be President, shared the same views on foreign policy and national defense, and had the ability to work with members of both parties in Congress in advancing administration programs. Ford then delivered a brief acceptance speech.

Ford's nomination was received favorably throughout the country and especially by members of both parties in Congress. Democratic Senator [Edward] Kennedy summed up the general reaction when he said that Ford had had "'an outstanding career and I foresee no difficulty whatever in his confirmation by the Senate.'" Said House Democratic Majority Whip [John] McFall: "'He should have no trouble at all.'" . . .

Action by the Senate

Following his nomination, Ford became the subject of the most extensive investigation accorded any candidate for national office. The Federal Bureau of Investigation dispatched more than 350 agents from thirty-three field offices to inquire into every aspect of his life. The Library of Congress concurrently undertook to make available to the committees of Congress all the information it could assemble on his life and public career. Staff personnel from the General Accounting Office and the Government Operations Permanent Investigations Subcommittee were made available to assist in the investigation. Ford's tax returns for the past seven years were examined, and those for the previous five were audited by the Internal Revenue Service and analyzed by the staffs of the House Judiciary Committee, the Senate Rules Committee, and the Joint Congressional Committee on Taxation. Ford's medical records were examined and persons who might have treated him questioned. Campaign reports, records, and statements on file with the House of Representatives and in Michigan were studied. His bank accounts, correspondence with government agencies, speeches, and office printing and payroll records were scrutinized; bar association and police records were examined for references to him.

As a result of this investigation, which included interviews with more than 1,000 persons, the FBI collected over 1700 pages of raw data which were inspected by the chairman and the ranking minority member of the Senate Rules Committee and the chairman and seven other members of the House Judiciary Committee. . . .

At the outset of the televised Senate hearings, Chairman Howard Cannon of Nevada stated that the "committee should view its obligations as no less important than the selection of a potential President of the United States." He expressed his view that under the Twenty-Fifth Amendment the President has the right to choose a person "whose philosophy and politics are virtually identical to his own," and that it is not proper to withhold confirmation based on a nominee's voting record in Congress. Rather, said Cannon, the committee's function was to examine a nominee's qualifications for Vice President— his morals, integrity, financial history, and the like. He concluded:

> It is for the members of this committee to establish a precedent—a solid, constitutional precedent—by pursuing an orderly, logical, thorough, and honest inquiry into the nominee's qualifications. This is being done in the public interest, because the citizens of the United States who normally choose the President and Vice President are participating only vicariously in this confirmation proceeding by following each action taken by the respective branches of the Congress. . . .

On November 20, thirty-eight days after beginning its inquiry, the Senate Rules and Administration Committee approved Ford's nomination, 9 to 0. In its report the committee said that not every member agreed with Ford's voting record, philosophy of government, personal and political views, and public actions during his twenty-five years in Congress, but judging him on his total record it saw no impediment which would disqualify him. The report stated that under the Twenty-Fifth Amendment a President would be expected to nominate a person of his own party and perhaps his own political philosophy. . . . In conclusion, the committee stated that in the critical areas of philosophy, character, and integrity, Ford "fully met reasonable tests."

Ford's nomination came to the floor of the Senate on November 27. The debate which followed was not extensive and reflected widespread support for Ford and little opposition. Democratic and Republican senators alike praised Ford's openness, candor, and integrity. A number of senators indicated that they would vote for confirmation despite their disagreement with his political philosophy. Democratic Senator Kennedy's remarks were typical:

> The nature of the 25th amendment is such that it intends not for the Senate to choose on its own a candidate for the Vice-Presidency who reflects the political beliefs of each Senator or of the body as a whole, but to "advise and consent" to the nomination of an individual. . . .

Throughout the debate senators acknowledged the possibility that Ford might become President. Thus, immediately after his nomination was approved, by a vote of 92 to 3, Senator [John] Tunney stated:

> Mr. Ford, within the next year, may, indeed, be President. So today's action not only initiates the 25th amendment of our Constitution, but may, in fact, ordain the 38th President of our Nation.

Action by the House

On November 15, the day after the Senate Rules Committee closed its public hearings, the thirty-eight-member House Judiciary Committee opened its televised hearings, with Gerald

Ford as the first witness. Almost half the witnesses who testified before the Senate Rules Committee also testified or submitted statements to the House Judiciary Committee. Prior to the commencement of the hearings, the House leadership made clear its determination that Ford's confirmation should not be delayed, as advocated by several members of the House, pending the outcome of the impeachment investigation; and that the confirmation hearings should be thorough so as to avoid charges of cronyism being leveled against the House. . . .

[An] area or disagreement involved the role of Congress under the Twenty-Fifth Amendment. Many accepted the view that the Amendment gave the President the right to choose a person who would be ideologically compatible with him. According to Representative [Edward] Hutchinson,

> the role of this committee is not to determine whether Gerald R. Ford's views on domestic and foreign policy are consonant with those of its members, but rather to determine whether he is qualified to assume the tensions and troubles of the Presidency if that office should for any reason devolve upon him, as well as to determine whether he is the kind of person in whom the people can place their trust.

Gerald Ford testified that

> the person so nominated must have a record that has been thoroughly investigated, that would justify the Congress and the American people in having faith and trust in his honesty, his experience, and his judgment. I think that is the criteria.

> The 25th amendment says nothing about the qualifications on a partisan basis or philosophical basis. . . .

Representatives [John] Conyers, Robert W. Kastenmeier of Wisconsin, and others thought it inappropriate for confirmation hearings to take place until the question of impeachment [of President Richard Nixon] had been settled. This led Representative [Robert] McClory to declare: "To suggest that we must await with the expectation or hope on the part of some that perhaps the President might be removed from office before acting to fill the office ... seems to me entirely erroneous and quite inappropriate. ..." The Amendment, said McClory, calls for an expeditious filling of the office of Vice President whenever it becomes vacant.

Ford's reputation in Congress and his conduct during the hearings provided a solid base for confirmation. As in the Senate hearings, members of both parties and witnesses constantly referred to his qualities of openness and honesty. While expressing his disapproval of Ford's civil rights record, Clarence Mitchell of the NAACP [National Association for the Advancement of Colored People] nevertheless stated that Ford was the "kind of person I would be glad to go on a hunting trip with; I know I would not get shot in the back." But, said Representative Michael Harrington of Massachusetts, "honesty and decency are not enough. We also must look for proven qualities of leadership and an ability to serve as a focal point around which a country, a troubled country as I view it, can rally." For Harrington, [Joseph L.] Rauh [Jr. of Americans for Democratic Action], and Mitchell, Ford did not possess these qualities. However, the image Ford presented at these televised hearings earned him accolades across the nation. Said [Representative Peter] Rodino: "With the question of candor before the public and so absolutely important and so much talked about, you certainly have displayed that kind of candor that has to be commended." ...

Debate and Confirmation

On December 6, 1973, the full House of Representatives took up Ford's nomination. During the almost six hours of debate, views were expressed similar to those aired at the hearings. A number of representatives said that they were voting in favor of confirmation on the basis of their understanding of the

Twenty-Fifth Amendment even though they differed with Ford's philosophy and voting record. Representative James O'Hara of Michigan said:

> I fail to see, in my reading of the 25th amendment, any requirement that the Congress withhold its consent to the nomination of a Vice President because his views are at variance with those of the majority of the Congress. I submit that to allow ourselves to be caught up in measuring Mr. Ford's qualifications for office against the subjective yardstick of our own philosophies would be to disserve the American people who expect Congress, at this critical moment in history, to rise above partisanship.

Numerous representatives expressed their admiration for Ford's candor, openness, integrity, and ability, and for his conduct during the most exhaustive and thorough investigation ever accorded a candidate for national office in American history. Experiences which members of Congress had shared with Ford during his twenty-five years as a member of the House were recited to show his qualifications for the vice presidency. "[A]t a time when many Americans are questioning the honesty of public officials and . . . have lost faith in those who serve in public office," said Robert E. Bauman of Maryland, "Gerald Ford's greatest attribute is his integrity." . . .

Throughout the House debates on Ford's nomination, unlike the Senate debates, differences of opinion were expressed concerning the intent of the Twenty-Fifth Amendment. Some said that it embodied a presumption in favor of the President's choice, and that it was improper to reject a nominee because his political philosophy was the same as the President's. Representative Conyers argued "that a Member of Congress should vote against . . . any nominee if in his judgment that nominee holds views or has a philosophy which when brought to that high office would in the judgment of the Congressman be unsatisfactory or harmful to the Nation as a whole." In response, Representative Charles E. Wiggins of California stated that such a standard would permit a repudiation of the popular mandate from the previous election. Added Wiggins: "It is my point of view ... that individual Members of Congress must rise against their personal notions of philosophy in order to maintain a continuity in the administration." ...

Several representatives argued that the Twenty-Fifth Amendment was never intended for the selection of a President, which they believed was occurring by virtue of the surrounding circumstances. Representative [Bella] Abzug said that there should be a special presidential election in the event of dual vacancies. Declared Representative Wiley Mayne of Iowa: "[T]hey [i.e., the dissenting members of the House Judiciary Committee] want to substitute some other method of choice than that which is provided in the 25th amendment. The hangup is that they want to abandon the 25th amendment and substitute a new and different method of choosing a Vice President." ...

After six hours of debate, Ford's nomination was favorably acted upon by a vote of 387 to 35. Among those voting against the nomination were the eight dissenting members of the House Judiciary Committee and a number of Democratic representatives of liberal persuasion. No Republican cast a negative vote.

Immediately following his confirmation as the fortieth Vice President, Ford was administered the vice presidential oath by Chief Justice Warren Burger before a joint meeting of the Congress held in the chamber of the House of Representatives. Among those in attendance were the justices of the Supreme Court, the members of the Cabinet, ambassadors and ministers of foreign countries, and President Nixon.

The Twenty-fifth Amendment Led to a Smooth Transfer of Power After President Nixon's Resignation

John F. Lawrence

John F. Lawrence was the Washington bureau chief for the Los Angeles Times. *In this report on Gerald Ford's succession to the presidency upon the 1974 resignation of Richard Nixon, he describes the smoothness of the transition. During the long Watergate scandal that led to Nixon's resignation, many people had become disillusioned with the American system of government and felt that the office of the president could no longer command respect. However, Lawrence points out, in contrast to power transfers in many other countries, Ford had no need to rally crowds or to call in military reinforcements to rebuild the government. In Lawrence's opinion, this demonstrates that the American system of government does indeed work.*

"My fellow Americans, our long national nightmare is over. Our Constitution works; our great republic is a government of laws and not of men. Here, the people rule."

With those words, the 38th President of the United States answered those who have been telling America for months that its system of government was somehow being jeopardized, that the office of the Presidency faced permanent damage.

It was an answer, too, to those who had characterized the long months of Watergate [the scandal that resulted in the resignation of President Richard Nixon] as a political struggle, as two political parties in something approaching mortal combat.

Occasions on Which the 25th Amendment Has Been Used

October 12, 1973	Gerald Ford was nominated as Vice President after Spiro Agnew's resignation
August 9, 1974	Gerald Ford became President after President Richard Nixon's resignation
August 20, 1974	Nelson Rockefeller was nominated as Vice President after Gerald Ford's succession to the presidency
July 13, 1985	George H. W. Bush became Acting President during President Ronald Reagan's surgery
June 29, 2002	Dick Cheney became Acting President during President George W. Bush's medical procedure
July 21, 2007	Dick Cheney again became Acting President during President George W. Bush's medical procedure

TAKEN FROM: Compiled by editor.

It was clear that President Ford believed that the nation had suffered a tragedy, but it was equally clear that he saw it a tragedy not of a government or of an office but of a man.

A Quiet Transfer of Power

Most of the week, unusual crowds had been gathering at the north gate of the White House, some with unfriendly signs, others part of a national organization that called itself bipartisan and claimed to be defending the Presidency.

Most of the people, however, were there just to look, to participate in their own way in the moment, the awesome shift in power taking place within the White House, their White House.

The quiet mood of that crowd said much about the transfer of power in this country. It spoke of contrast with the picture of surging mobs, shouted slogans and frenzied speeches from balconies that accompany so many sudden shifts of power in so many other lands.

Inside the White House, the ceremony was incredibly simple, as always, designed to remind the central figure in it that his power flows primarily from a document written years ago, not from the crowd of the moment.

As the 38th President turned to the official gathering in the East Room to speak, it became clear once again what differentiates the American Presidency from positions that bear the same title in other countries.

It was that Gerald R. Ford had no need to go to the balcony to rally the crowd, to call out the military to rebuild the power of a shattered government. Political opponents he had—some with ambition to stand where he stood. But enemies he had not.

As he spoke for the first time as President, suddenly there was greatness in his words. The man so many have called a nice man flashed something extra in wisdom, in strength and, perhaps most welcome of all, in sense of good taste.

And as he spoke, life in the nation went on, barely pausing to witness the event.

A visitor to Washington's National Airport at precisely the hour of noon Friday was struck by the sight of busy people deplaning, entering the terminal and then suddenly confronting a hushed atmosphere. The normally bustling crowds had stopped to watch small television screens at scattered points in the waiting room.

It was at that moment that the leadership of the Western world was passing into new hands. And some of the travelers, preoccupied with schedules and baggage and taxis, clearly had forgotten.

Perhaps that said it all. They cared, certainly, but they were not seriously concerned. The Presidency had not fallen. Only a President.

Nelson Rockefeller Was the Second Vice President Appointed Under the Twenty-fifth Amendment

Alvin S. Felzenburg

Alvin S. Felzenburg teaches at the Annenberg School for Communication at the University of Pennsylvania. He was the principal spokesman for the 9/11 Commission and has served in several senior staff positions in the U.S. House of Representatives. In this excerpt from an article about the vice presidency, he describes the nomination of Nelson Rockefeller to be vice president after Gerald Ford succeeded to the presidency. Rockefeller, who had been a candidate for the Republication nomination for president in several past elections, hoped that as vice president he would have a position of influence; but the reality fell short of his expectations, Felzenburg states, despite promises from Ford. He was delayed in assuming office by an exceptionally long series of confirmation hearings, and his views were in conflict with those of many members of his own party. Nevertheless, Felzenburg says, he was a valuable adviser to Ford, and the office of vice president gained increased prestige during his tenure.

The vice presidency took on increased importance in the aftermath of Watergate. Gerald Ford, the first vice president appointed to his post and confirmed by both houses of Congress under the terms of the Twenty-Fifth Amendment, used his nine months in office to prepare himself for the presidency. He had gone into the post aware that the odds were strong that [Richard] Nixon would vacate the office before the end of his term. Days before Nixon's resignation, Ford announced that he would cease defending Nixon and refrain from all comment on matters pertaining to Watergate [the scandal that caused Nixon to resign], another indication of the fast-approaching end.

Once in office, Ford surprised his friends and angered his opponents when he announced his intention to appoint Nelson Rockefeller as vice president. After the instability that had beset the executive branch with the second resignation of a vice president and the first of a president in American history, Ford wanted to convey that he would be serving with someone universally deemed ready to become president.

Rockefeller, having been elected New York's governor four times, with service in the State Department under FDR [Franklin Delano Roosevelt] and Ike [Dwight D. Eisenhower] also under his belt, was certainly that. Rockefeller had competed for the GOP [Republican Party] presidential nomination in 1960 and 1968 and was preparing to run in 1976. Rockefeller had previously declined the second spot, arguing that he had never "wanted to be vice president of anything."

Yet he agreed to serve, because he shared Ford's concern that the nation and the world needed assurance that the American system of leadership was stable. His major condition was that he be named chairman of the Domestic Council—where he would, in the domestic field, command influence of the kind his protégé Henry Kissinger [Nixon's secretary of state] held over foreign policy.

Prolonged Confirmation

Although Ford kept his promise, Rockefeller's hopes went unfulfilled. First he fell victim to a prolonged confirmation hearing in which leftist activists probed the Rockefeller family fortune. That delayed him from taking command of his post at the outset of Ford's administration. Once there, he found himself at loggerheads with other members of the president's

President Gerald Ford delivers his first State of the Union Address. He is backed by Vice President Nelson Rockefeller, the second vice president to be appointed under the Twenty-fifth Amendment, and Speaker of the House Carl Albert. AP Images.

team who either saw him as a rival to their own ambitions or at odds with the administration's policies.

With inflation and unemployment growing and Ford embarked on a veto strategy against the overwhelmingly liberal Democratic "Watergate Congress," the administration was not about to embrace costly initiatives of the kind Rockefeller was proposing. Moreover, Rockefeller's record as governor, which was decidedly liberal on both spending and social policy, earned him the wrath of party conservatives. Rockefeller further antagonized conservatives when he ruled from the Senate's presiding chair that a vote by simple majority rather than two-thirds could end filibusters. In the face of Ronald Reagan's hefty and spirited challenge in the primaries [preceding the 1976 presidential election], Ford concluded that Rockefeller was a political liability and dropped him from his ticket months in advance of the 1976 convention.

Despite his frustrations in the policy arena, Rockefeller, because of his connections all over the world and independent sources of information, proved a valuable adviser to Ford. While he failed to persuade Ford to embrace most of his ideas, Rockefeller did provide information and advice to the president during weekly private lunches. This Ford-Rockefeller innovation became a part of the routine for every president and vice president since.

The office of the vice president also enjoyed enhanced ceremonial prestige during Rockefeller's abbreviated tenure. He designed its coat of arms and flag and pressed for and obtained the establishment of an official vice presidential residence, which he was the first to occupy.

The Twenty-fifth Amendment Was Not Invoked When President Ronald Reagan Was Shot

The Los Angeles Times

This report from the Los Angeles Times *discusses the issue of whether the Twenty-fifth Amendment should have been used in 1981 when President Ronald Reagan was shot during an assassination attempt. Looking back on the events, Reagan's physician suggests that it should have been, the reporter says. The physician explains that it did not occur to him to suggest to Reagan's aides that the amendment be invoked because he was preoccupied by concern for his patient. The president underwent emergency surgery and was in the recovery room for several days. Testimony to a study commission and other statements from officials who were present confirm that there was a state of confusion at the White House after Reagan's shooting. According to the author, some Cabinet members did not even know about the Twenty-fifth Amendment.*

Ronald Reagan's White House physician said Monday [February 20, 1989,] he now believes that executive power should have been transferred to then-Vice President George [H.W.] Bush after Reagan was shot on March 30, 1981.

Daniel Ruge said that in hindsight, the emergency provisions of the 25th Amendment allowing for the transfer of authority should have been invoked after the assassination attempt.

The doctor, now living in retirement in Denver, said: "I knew all about" the 25th Amendment, "but it never occurred to me" to suggest to Reagan's aides that it be invoked.

As White House physician, he kept a copy of the 25th Amendment in his bag, Ruge said in a telephone interview from his home.

But in the hours after Reagan was shot in the chest by John W. Hinckley Jr. outside a Washington hotel, Ruge said he was preoccupied with the President's condition.

Concerned with His Patient

"Any physician should be more interested in his patient," Ruge said. "I have no apologies to make."

At the time of the shooting, Bush was traveling in Texas. He returned to Washington immediately.

But testimony to a University of Virginia study commission, and statements by officials who were present at the time, confirmed that a general state of confusion existed at the White House after Reagan's shooting.

There was no clear attempt to address the question of transferring power during the time that Reagan was undergoing emergency surgery to remove a bullet from a lung, or in the several days after when he was in a recovery room at George Washington University Medical Center.

"Somebody should have been looking after the store" during that period, Ruge said, but "fortunately, everything went well. The country moved forward."

The former White House physician's remarks were initially reported in Monday's *New York Times*.

The White House atmosphere in the hours immediately following Reagan's shooting was dramatized by the now-famous statement by then-Secretary of State Alexander M. Haig Jr., who proclaimed to reporters: "As of now, I am in control here, in the White House, pending the return of the vice president."

Section 3 of the 25th Amendment, ratified in 1967, four years after President John F. Kennedy's assassination, provides for a temporary transfer of executive power to the vice president.

The power remains with the vice president until the President sends a letter to leaders of Congress certifying that he is ready to resume authority.

Fred Fielding, who was Reagan's chief White House counsel at the time, could not be reached for comment Monday.

Fielding, however, told the University of Virginia study commission that, "to be very frank with you, that day, when I mentioned the 25th Amendment, I could see eyes glazing over in some parts of the Cabinet. They didn't even know about the 25th Amendment."

Reagan signed a letter to Capitol Hill leaders in 1985, at the time of his colon cancer surgery, saying he was relinquishing power to Bush during the time he was under general anesthesia.

But White House officials did not actually invoke Section 3 of the 25th Amendment on that occasion.

In a *New York Times* interview shortly before his [presidential] inauguration [in 1989], Bush said that "it never occurred to me" to discuss the 25th Amendment with his campaign running mate, Dan Quayle, now the vice president.

Deputy White House Press Secretary Steven Hart said Monday that a book, "Contingency Plan for Transfer of Presidential Authority," was compiled in the Reagan White House and has been "updated" by the Bush Administration.

President Ronald Reagan Temporarily Transferred Power to the Vice President Before Undergoing Anesthesia

Fred F. Fielding

Fred F. Fielding, an attorney, was counsel to President Ronald Reagan. In the following excerpt from testimony to a commission studying the issue of presidential disability, he describes how Reagan turned his power over to Vice President George H.W. Bush before undergoing anesthesia for minor surgery in 1985. Reagan did not formally invoke the Twenty-fifth Amendment on this occasion. He merely followed the procedure it specifies of sending a letter to Congress informing them of the transfer of power, and he sent another letter when he was ready to resume his duties. Fielding acknowledges that there were some questions about whether Reagan returned too soon after surgery, but Fielding discussed it with the surgeon, who said that Reagan was lucid. Advisers felt that the public needed reassurance that the president was in good condition.

Let's go back to the week before the operation. We knew—some of us knew—and I forget when it became public, that the President was going to have his physical. We knew at the time that he was going to have a form of anaesthesia, to have the procedure that occurred on Friday, if I recall my dates correctly. He was operated on on Saturday, got a procedure on Friday. What was going to happen was that there was a possibility that if something was found that they would have to instantly put the President under. I used that as an oppor-

Fred F. Fielding, *Papers on Presidential Disability and the Twenty-Fifth Amendment*, Lanham, MD: University Press of America and The Miller Center, 1997. Copyright © 1997 by University Press of America, Inc. All rights reserved. Reproduced by permission.

tunity the preceding week to schedule a meeting with the President and the Vice President and Don Regan (then chief of staff). We sat in the Oval Office and we discussed the whole situation: the National Command Authority plus the President's desires on passage of power temporarily if he were suddenly temporarily incapacitated. . . .

The decision was obvious that unless something unexpected occurred on Friday there would be no need for the Twenty-fifth Amendment in any shape or form. But Don Regan called me down later [in the] afternoon on that Friday and said, "We've got some problems with the health exam." And we went through the whole drill—if you will—of what is to be done and where is the Vice President, what is the press to be advised and what is not to be told, and the normal procedures that you go through. One of the subjects obviously was the Twenty-fifth Amendment. I can tell you, and I think it is important for the sake of history, that when we left, no decision of a recommendation to the President had been made although we knew the procedures. I drafted basically two letters: One was a little fleshing out of the letter that was already in the book, and the other was basically the letter the President actually signed. I did that because I knew that there was reluctance on the part of the President to activate the Twenty-fifth Amendment for a "minor" procedure of short-term duration. . . .

Two Options

I thought the President should have two options: One was very clear, that of the exercise of the Twenty-fifth Amendment; and the other was a piece that would accomplish the activation of the Twenty-fifth Amendment but was more consistent with what I perceived to be the President's concerns. His concern mainly was that he didn't want to set a precedent for future presidents. But I can tell you in all candor there was no political reason why he didn't want to, which theoretically there could be as with someone who is having a power fight or whatever you would with their Vice President.

Next morning I sat down with the Chief of Staff at the hospital and we discussed this. I showed him the two drafts, the normal draft and the optional draft, and I don't think Don's mind was made up at that point, until that point, to be very honest. I think his mind was still open about it. We discussed it and then we went in and discussed it with the President in the hospital room. And he made his decision; he signed the optional paper. As it turned out, the doctor had predicted three hours for the operation. He wanted to get a little head start, so he started the anaesthesia earlier than he had told us he was going to start it because he wanted to give himself a little more time. So there probably was a period of time in there, although it was academic, a technical period of time when the President was out, and we had not called Vice President [George H.W.] Bush.

Later that afternoon we asked to see the [surgeon]. We explained to him the Twenty-fifth Amendment, the implications of it. We explored it with him. I was asking questions about how you could know, what was the legitimate way to determine whether the President was capable, understanding, lucid, and that sort of thing. We hit upon several tests, one of which was that I said "I'm going to ask him to sign a letter. How about asking him to read the letter and understand it? Wouldn't that be evidence that he was lucid?" And he said, "Yep." We went in a little after seven to see him. He was joking with the nurses when we walked in. We had a conversation with him; we discussed the transfer of power. I handed him the letter and he picked it up and literally started to read it and his eyes were shutting and opening, and it was obviously going like this, like he was turning his eyes. And I thought, uh oh, and Don Regan and I looked at each other and decided that maybe we were a little premature. Then the President reminded us that he didn't have his glasses and he didn't have his contacts on and he couldn't read it. It had nothing to do with his consciousness at all. We read the letter to him; we discussed it with him. Don said something, in effect, "Now that you know what we are up to, Mr. President, maybe we'll come back in a couple of hours and ask you to sign it," when at that point the President said (this is not a full quote, but something to the effect), "Oh, heck no, I don't want you to wake me up later. I'll sign it now." So we decided he was lucid enough, certainly, to take [the power of the president] back.

Reclaiming Presidential Powers

My mind was that [the transfer of power] should not be shorter than necessary or longer than required since this was the first exercise of the Amendment. I would have had no problem with going overnight with everything we knew and all the briefings that we had and all the strategic information we had. But in my mind, again, my own personal view was if you were comfortable with the President's condition, the sooner the better for any number of reasons. And certainly it was a very practical, political reason that the public out there needed reassurance the President was in fact really O.K., this wasn't a death-threatening situation, that . . . he had come through the procedure and was lucid enough to take back the problems.

The worst thing in the world would have been to have him transfer—and this was the other thing we talked about— the power to the Vice President, take it back, and then later have to transfer it back again. So that was a factor in our thinking as well. We had to be reassured by the doctors that the probabilities of that to occur were low.

Our question was not, was the man in discomfort? The question was whether he was lucid or whether he had the ability to carry on, not whether it was comfortable in the short term. When somebody asked whether the White House physician was in on the discussion, the answer was no. But I

Before surgery, President Ronald Reagan temporarily transferred his powers to Vice President George H.W. Bush, without officially invoking the Twenty-fifth Amendment. © Betmann/Corbis.

know that Don Regan talked to the doctor at that time and we had discussed the scenario with him the night before. It wasn't that the White House physician was excluded; it was that once we got into the surgery phase that we were dealing with the surgical team.

President George W. Bush Invoked the Twenty-fifth Amendment Before Undergoing Anesthesia

Associated Press

The following selection describes President George W. Bush's invocation of the Twenty-fifth Amendment to transfer the powers of his office to Vice President Dick Cheney during a 2007 medical procedure that required anesthesia. He did this "out of an abundance of caution," said the White House spokesperson, due to the war in Iraq and terrorist threats; the actual time under anesthetic was very short. Five years previously, the author points out, Bush had undergone the same procedure and had invoked the amendment then as well.

Doctors removed five small growths from President [George W.] Bush's colon Saturday [July 21, 2007,] after he temporarily transferred the powers of his office to Vice President Dick Cheney under the rarely invoked 25th Amendment.

The polyps, extra tissue growing inside the large intestine, were found during a routine colon cancer scan performed at the Camp David presidential retreat.

"All were less than 1 centimeter (about four-tenths of an inch) and none appeared worrisome," White House spokesman Scott Stanzel said. Outside medical experts agreed.

The polyps were sent to the National Naval Medical Center in Bethesda, Md., to be microscopically examined for signs of cancer. Results were expected in 48 to 72 hours. Polyps can turn cancerous, so finding them early is one of the best ways to prevent the disease and improve the odds of surviving it.

"The standard procedure is to remove all polyps that you see," said Dr. David Weinberg, director of gastroenterology at Fox Chase Cancer Center in Philadelphia, who was not part of the medical team at Camp David. "But the majority of polyps taken out that are less than 1 centimeter in size are very unlikely to have cancer in them."

No Actions Taken by Cheney

Bush invoked the presidential disability clause of the Constitution at 7:16 a.m. EDT. He transferred his authority to Cheney, who was at his home on the Chesapeake Bay in St. Michaels, Md., about 45 miles east of Washington.

Nothing occurred during the 2 hours and 5 minutes of the transfer that required Cheney to take official action, Stanzel said.

First lady Laura Bush was in Midland, Texas, celebrating her mother's birthday. The president spoke with her by phone before and after the colonoscopy.

Stanzel said the exam was performed under what he called "monitored anesthesia care," not general anesthesia. Under general anesthesia, a patient loses consciousness. Stanzel said Bush was asleep but responsive during the colon check. The medical team stopped administering anesthesia at 7:41 a.m. EDT; Bush was up 3 minutes later.

During the 31-minute procedure, Bush was sedated with a drug called propofol.

"The advantage is that it works faster and wears off considerably faster than the standard agents," Weinberg said. He said some other drugs can leave a person groggy for hours after a colonoscopy.

After the examination, Bush ate breakfast with chief of staff Joshua Bolten, White House counsel Fred Fielding and national security adviser Stephen Hadley. He played with his dogs, rode his bike in the afternoon for more than an hour around the presidential compound in the Catoctin Mountains of western Maryland, and received informal briefings from Bolten and Hadley.

"The president was in good humor and will resume his normal activities at Camp David," Stanzel said.

Dr. Richard Tubb, the president's doctor, supervised the colonoscopy, performed by a team from the Bethesda medical center.

For the general population, a colonoscopy to screen for colon cancer is recommended every 10 years. But for people at higher risk, or if a colonoscopy detects polyps, follow-up colonoscopies often are scheduled in three- to five-year intervals.

Doctors discovered that Bush had two polyps during a similar scan in 1998 and two more were found during a colon screening in 1999, while Bush was governor of Texas. That made the 61-year-old president a prime candidate for regular examinations. The screening done in 2002 revealed no polyps or abnormalities.

"The more polyps you have, the more frequently you need to have a colonoscopy," said Dr. Roshini Rajapaksa, a gastroenterologist at New York University Medical Center who was not involved in the exam. "But because they're small in size, it's not that worrisome even though he had five." . . .

'An Abundance of Caution'

Given the war in Iraq and terrorist threats across the world, the president invoked Section 3 of the 25th Amendment "out of an abundance of caution," Stanzel said. The amendment, approved in 1967, four years after President Kennedy was assassinated, provides for the temporary or permanent transfer of presidential power in case the president is unable to fulfill the duties of the office.

It had been used only twice before.

In July 1985, President Reagan had colon cancer surgery and turned over power to his vice president, George H.W. Bush. During the president's colorectal screening on July 29, 2002, Bush relinquished powers to Cheney for more than two hours.

This transfer of power took place with letters Bush faxed to House Speaker Nancy Pelosi, D-Calif., and Sen. Robert Byrd, D-W.Va., president pro tempore of the Senate. Bush reclaimed his authority at 9:21 a.m. EDT with follow-up letters to both lawmakers.

"This letter shall constitute my written declaration that I am presently able to resume the discharge of the Constitutional powers and duties of the office of the president of the United States," Bush's one-paragraph letter said.

Limitations of the Twenty-fifth Amendment

The Twenty-fifth Amendment Needs Clarification in Regard to Presidential Succession

Antonin Scalia

Antonin Scalia is now a justice of the U.S. Supreme Court, but he was an assistant attorney general when he presented this statement during a hearing held by the U.S. Senate Subcommittee on Constitutional Amendments. In that statement, he asserts that there are serious difficulties in the relationship between the Twenty-fifth Amendment and the Presidential Succession Act. It is not clear whether a substitute vice president can be nominated by a person who is an acting president under the statute. Also, Scalia says, there is no consideration of what would happen if a president died after nominating a new vice president who had not yet been confirmed. A further ambiguity pointed out by Scalia concerns the question of whether acting replacements for cabinet members can participate in determining presidential inability.

The relationship between the Twenty-fifth Amendment and the Presidential Succession Act of 1947, poses some serious difficulties. This statute was enacted pursuant to the constitutional provision that "the Congress may by law provide for the case of removal, death, resignation, or inability, both of the President and Vice President, declaring what officer shall then act as President, and such officer shall act accordingly, until the disability be removed, or a President shall be elected." The statutory implementation of this provision estab-

Antonin Scalia, "Twenty-Fifth Amendment Proposals Aired in Senate Hearings; Association Position Favors No Changes," *American Bar Association Journal*, May 1975, pp. 603–604.

lishes an order of succession which consists of the Speaker of the House, the president pro tempore of the Senate, and then cabinet officers beginning with the secretary of state.

The first question posed by the intersection of this provision with the Twenty-fifth Amendment is whether the amendment can be invoked by a person who is an acting president under the statute. That is, assuming that both the president and vice president are killed in a single catastrophe, can the Speaker of the House nominate a person to become vice president? The scant legislative history on this point appears to indicate that the answer is "no." This seems to me the most satisfactory conclusion, since one of the essential features of the amendment is eliminated when the nominating president cannot trace his tenure to a political mandate from the entire electorate.

A Potential Conflict

Another series of questions is posed when, after the amendment's machinery has already been set in motion, the incumbent president dies without a vice president in office. That is, once a president has forwarded a nomination under the amendment to fill a vacancy in the vice presidency, will the Speaker of the House become the acting president if the president dies before congressional action on the nomination? The legislative history of the amendment is again scant on the point, but the answer appears to be "yes."

The issue then raised, assuming that the Speaker has become acting president, is his relationship to the already initiated Twenty-fifth Amendment process. Need he, or indeed can he, withdraw the nomination? If the nomination subsists and is approved, will the vice president thereby created displace the Speaker and become president? There is no clear answer to these questions in the legislative history of the amendment, but the portions referred to with respect to the earlier questions seem to display an assumption that once the nominating president dies, the entire Twenty-fifth Amendment process is terminated and thereafter only the Presidential Succession Act controls. I am of the view that this is the preferable disposition.

Any theory which would allow the nomination to subsist should also lead to the conclusion that the nominee, if approved, not only becomes vice president but thereupon immediately supplants the Speaker as president. (Otherwise there would be created a vice president who has more apparent entitlement than the acting president to the post of chief executive.) This would have the result of making the Speaker merely a caretaker president during whatever period is required for congressional approval of his successor. . . .

The original scheme of the Constitution was that there should always be a person ready to assume the duties of the presidency for the balance of the unexpired term; there is nothing to indicate that the Twenty-fifth Amendment was meant to alter that basic disposition. It might also be pointed out that the Speaker of the House or the president pro tempore of the Senate must resign his post in order to become acting president under the Succession Act; they would have little inclination to do so if the nomination of their successor remained pending.

It is true that the customary practice with respect to nominations by a deceased president appears to be that they subsist without the necessity of renewal by his successor. But a nomination under the Twenty-fifth Amendment is a sufficiently distinctive act to justify a contrary practice. Indeed, if the normal practice were followed a number of irrational variables would be introduced—such as the fact that under present . . . Senate Standing Rules all nominations terminate at the end of a session, and when the Senate recesses for more than thirty days. . . . It seems clearly undesirable to make the applicability of the Twenty-fifth Amendment depend upon such irrelevant factors, and this is an additional reason for adopting the view

---

Presidential Line of Succession

1. Vice President of the United States
2. Speaker of the House of Representatives
3. President Pro Tempore of the Senate
4. Secretary of State
5. Secretary of the Treasury
6. Secretary of Defense
7. Attorney General
8. Secretary of the Interior
9. Secretary of Agriculture
10. Secretary of Commerce
11. Secretary of Labor
12. Secretary of Health and Human Services
13. Secretary of Housing and Urban Development
14. Secretary of Transportation
15. Secretary of Energy
16. Secretary of Education
17. Secretary of Veterans Affairs
18. Secretary of Homeland Security

TAKEN FROM: Compiled by editor.

---

that upon death of the nominating president the amendment's process invariably comes to an end, and the Presidential Succession Act thereafter governs. . . .

I urge the subcommittee to consider amending the Presidential Succession Act in such manner as to clarify its relationship with the Twenty-fifth Amendment as described above. . . .

Who Determines Disability?

Another issue which remains obscure under the Twenty-fifth Amendment—though unlike those discussed above, it has not yet been raised in a practical context—is the question of who may participate in a determination of presidential disability under Section 4 of the amendment. That section covers situations in which the ailing president is unwilling or unable to declare his own inability to discharge the powers and duties of his office. In such event, a declaration of such inability can be made to the Congress by "a majority of either the principal officers of the executive departments or of such other body as Congress may by law provide." Upon such declaration, the vice president assumes the presidential functions and retains them until the president transmits to the Congress his written declaration that no inability exists (with provision for rejection of such declaration by the Congress, in the event of an opposing declaration by the vice president and, once again, "a majority of either the principal officers of the executive departments or of such other body as Congress may by law provide").

Congress has made no provision for a body to exercise this constitutional function of determining presidential inability, so the determination now rests with "a majority of the principal officers of the executive departments." The important issue which requires clarification is whether this phrase includes a Cabinet member's acting replacement (his undersecretary, the deputy attorney general, or other designated official) in the event the Cabinet member himself has died, resigned, or is sick or absent. Such substitution is the rule with respect to other functions of the Cabinet members. The statute governing the Justice Department, for example, provides that when the office of attorney general is vacant, "the deputy attorney general may exercise all the duties of that office." But such statutes cannot be dispositive with respect to constitutionally prescribed functions; there the intent of the Constitution itself must govern.

With respect to this intent, there is a direct conflict between the House report on the proposed Twenty-fifth Amendment, which stated that the acting head of a department would be authorized to participate, and the Senate floor manager, Senator [Birch] Bayh, who in the floor debate expressed his opinion that an acting head could not participate. As a matter of statutory construction, it is exceedingly difficult to predict how the Supreme Court would choose between these two highly authoritative indicia of legislative intent.

With respect to this particular problem, it is simple for the Congress by statute to provide a clear and dispositive solution. Whatever the phrase "principal officers of the executive departments" may mean, it is clear under the amendment that the necessary determination can be made by "such other body as Congress may by law provide." I urge you to consider recommending adoption of a provision which would specify that the determination of disability is to be made by Cabinet secretaries only—or, if you wish, by Cabinet secretaries or their replacements.

I tend to favor the former because of the possibility that a Cabinet secretary's first assistant (not to mention a more junior assistant, if he should succeed to the vacancy) will be overly deferential to both the president and the other Cabinet secretaries, with the result that his judgment will not be as bold and independent as it should be. Moreover, there is something to be said for the proposition that in order to tell when the president is sick, it helps to have known him well when he was healthy. Those below the Cabinet level may not possess this qualification.

But my preference on this point is only a mild one. The nature of the choice is less important than the making of it. What is crucial is that a clear answer be provided before the constitutional provision must be used.

The Twenty-fifth Amendment's Provision for Dealing with Presidential Illness Is Inadequate

Kenneth R. Crispell and Carlos F. Gomez

When the following viewpoint was written, Kenneth R. Crispell was an emeritus professor of medicine and law at the University of Virginia, and Carlos F. Gomez was a medical student pursuing a doctorate in public policy studies. This selection is based on their book Hidden Illness in the White House. *In it the authors point out a number of uncertainties in the Twenty-fifth Amendment. For instance, the Constitution does not spell out how to determine presidential disability. They also argue that although the Twenty-fifth Amendment specifies a procedure to use in the case of disability, it does not ensure that the amendment will be invoked. Furthermore, in the authors' opinion it would take too long to remove a disabled president against his will. The president's physician would face a conflict between his obligations to patient confidentiality and to national security. Crispell and Gomez feel the best solution to these problems would be for each president to prepare a written protocol to be followed if he becomes ill.*

On the morning of July 13, 1985, Ronald Reagan awoke in his hospital bed at Bethesda Naval Hospital, in Maryland, and prepared to undergo surgery to remove a polyp that had been discovered in his colon the day before. The three-hour operation would be routine but debilitating: . . . The immediate problem facing administration officials that Saturday was how to prepare for the several hours during which the

Reprinted with the permission of the New York Academy of Sciences, 7 World Trade Center, 250 Greenwich Str., 40th Floor, New York, NY 10007. www.nyas.org.

President would be unconscious. Unlike most people in the same situation, he could not simply excuse himself from his responsibilities for the day. He had to prepare for the possibility, however remote, that immediate presidential action might be required—that terrorists might take American citizens hostage, that nuclear war might break out somewhere in the world, that the United States itself might come under attack.

The Constitution contains a provision for dealing with such situations: Section three of the Twenty-fifth Amendment specifies that the President shall inform the President Pro Tempore of the Senate and the Speaker of the House of Representatives, in writing whenever he will be temporarily unable to serve, so that the powers and duties of his office can be delegated to the Vice-President. The President can reclaim his responsibilities, when he judges himself ready, by again notifying the two leaders of Congress. In essence, Reagan decided to follow this procedure—though, in an attempt to downplay the seriousness of his incapacity, he stated that he was not formally *invoking* the Twenty-fifth Amendment but only following a long-standing informal arrangement with Vice-President George [H.W.] Bush. . . . It was the first such delegation of power in U.S. history.

Surgery began at 11:48 A.M., and at 7:22 that evening, on the advice of Chief of Staff Donald Regan and White House Counsel Fred Fielding, Reagan sent letters to [Speaker Tip] O'Neill and [president pro tempore Senator Strom] Thurmond declaring himself "able to resume the discharge of the constitutional powers and duties of the office of the President of the United States." Given that, only five hours earlier, he had been under the numbing effects of spinal anesthesia, that his body had just suffered the shock of major surgery, and that he was receiving periodic injections of narcotics to reduce pain, one wonders about the wisdom of such a hasty decision. Any postoperative patient undergoes substantial metabolic changes, and experiences quite noticeable mental fatigue and

The first president to share full details of his illness with the American public, President Dwight D. Eisenhower outlined procedures he wished Vice President Richard Nixon to follow should he suffer permanent disability, establishing the pattern that led to the Twenty-fifth Amendment. © Betmann/Corbis.

disorientation. Yet, according to Fielding, at the time the decision was made, the President's surgeons had said "everything was fine" and had pronounced the President "alert." Perhaps, in their eagerness to reassure themselves and the White House staff, they failed to realize that their statements stood a chance of changing history. . . .

Defining Presidential Disability

What did the Constitution mean when it spoke of a President's "inability"? Who would determine whether any such inability existed? How could a President in this condition be removed? And under what circumstances might he resume office?

If the first thirty-nine Presidents were able to avoid these issues, it was not because they were all perfectly healthy but because their medical problems were kept secret. . . .

The first time the American public immediately knew the full truth about a President's illness was during the administration of Dwight D. Eisenhower. While still in his first term of office, Eisenhower suffered from three major illnesses. . . .

By the time his third illness struck, Eisenhower recognized the need for some arrangement in the event he suffered permanent disability. He issued a private letter to Vice-President Richard M. Nixon outlining procedures to be followed if such a problem should occur. The letter provided that the President would declare his own inability, if he could, and, if not, the Vice-President, "after appropriate consultation" (with whom, the letter did not say), would. In either event, the Vice-President was to serve as *Acting* President until such time as the President resumed the powers and duties of office by declaring himself fit again. It was a cautious, but important, step toward filling the constitutional void.

President John F. Kennedy continued this practice, specifying the cabinet as the "appropriate" body for consultation. And President Lyndon B. Johnson, first with House Speaker John W. McCormack (from the time Kennedy was assassinated, in 1963, until the next Vice-President, Hubert H. Humphrey, was sworn in, in 1965) and then with Humphrey, reached similar agreements. In the meantime, spurred by the specter of Eisenhower's illnesses, Congress set in motion the hearings that would lead to the passage of the Twenty-fifth Amendment, in 1964, and its ratification by the states in 1967. . . .

Uncertainties in the Amendment

The Twenty-fifth Amendment . . . provides a much more detailed prescription for dealing with presidential death and illness than there ever had been. But it is still thus short of ensuring that no matter what illness or accident befalls a President or a Vice-President, the powers and duties of the Chief Executive's office will methodically be passed along to a qualified replacement. For one thing, as the episode of Reagan's colon surgery illustrated, there is nothing in the amendment that ensures it will even be invoked in all cases of presidential illness. Reagan's decision *not* to invoke the amendment suggests that other Presidents, too, may shy away from it for fear of sending too strong a message that something is wrong in the White House. Moreover, the amendment does not anticipate every case in which a transfer of presidential power might be needed. For instance, it has no provision for a situation in which a Vice-President becomes ill and unable to serve; it says only that he can be replaced in the event of death, resignation, or removal from office. It also fails to address cases of long-term presidential disability in which the Vice-President acts as President, leaving a vacancy of uncertain duration in the office of Vice-President. And there are no provisions for the simultaneous incapacity of President and Vice-President. Presumably, the line of succession specified in the Presidential Succession Act would become operative in such situations.

There is also the question of whether the procedure for removing a disabled President against his will is efficient enough. Can the nation afford to tolerate a period of three weeks for Congress to decide whether a President is able to serve? And should there not be some limitation on the number of times a President who has been relieved of his duties can challenge the decision? Until the end of the Second World War, one might have supposed that even a delay of several weeks in the transference of command, while debilitating, could be tolerated. But in this age of nuclear weapons, it is extremely critical that, at all times, presidential power be in the hands of a competent leader who can respond quickly.

There is little chance that Congress will clear up these technical uncertainties in the Twenty-fifth Amendment anytime soon. Legislators who were in office at the time the amendment was debated report that all the questions it raises were acknowledged even then. But members of both parties were reluctant to make the law detailed, for fear it would somehow tie the hands of the people who had to respond to presidential illness. Thus, it will remain largely up to the individuals involved in any particular instance of presidential disability—especially the Vice-President and the President's physician—to be aware of the problems and make certain that the office is transferred smoothly and quickly to the next person in line.

Patient Confidentiality vs. National Security

In any case of presidential illness, it is likely to be difficult to know for sure when the Chief Executive has become "unable to discharge the powers and duties of his office." Naturally, the authors of the amendment could not specify the great variety of physical and mental afflictions that might render a President incapable of operating effectively, so each instance must be evaluated separately. But at present, there are no guidelines for how this evaluation ought to take place. As Reagan's experience demonstrates, whether the President considers removing himself from office or other officials contemplate doing it for him, the decision is likely to be difficult.

The procedure for removing a President from office is essentially a political one, but it must be based upon medical advice. Theoretically, this places the White House physician in a powerful position. In reality, however, he has minimal responsibilities. . . .

Of course, in consulting the physician, presidential advisers must be able to trust that he will give them sound advice. Historically, though, the President's physician has considered his first responsibility to be not the welfare of the nation but the health of his patient. Admiral [Cary] Grayson went to extreme lengths to hide Woodrow Wilson's illness from the cabinet, Congress, and the public. Even Mrs. Wilson was not given all the facts. Admiral [Ross] McIntire was likewise successful in keeping secret the seriousness of FDR's [Franklin Delano Roosevelt's] ill health. Both cases demonstrate that the White House physician, like all physicians, is, by custom, inclined to keep the state of his patient's health confidential. In 1957, the American Medical Association included in its code of ethics a statement advising physicians to betray a patient's confidence if "it becomes necessary in order to protect the individual or the community." Whether this will suffice to compel future White House physicians to break *their* patients' confidences remains an open question.

Beyond this ethical obligation, the President's physician may have some legal obligation to put national security ahead of patient confidentiality—if specifically called upon by Congress to do so. On the basis of Supreme Court decisions on the extent to which conversations between the President and his advisers may be kept secret, Paul Stephan, of the University of Virginia School of Law, has concluded that, although Congress could not routinely monitor private consultations between the President and his physician, it could compel the physician to testify about the President's condition if there were a specific reason to suspect that the Chief Executive was seriously ill. This does not offer an especially efficient means of monitoring the President's health, however, because there is no guarantee that Congress would know when a President was suffering from a potentially incapacitating illness.

Suggested Solutions

In view of the traditional difficulty of getting information from the White House physician, it has been suggested, at various times, that questions of a President's ability to serve should be referred to a panel of medical experts. . . .

The trouble with such panels, and the reason they never have been instituted, is that they would deny the President a privilege that most of us treasure: the privilege of keeping counsel with one's own, personally selected physician. And such a drastic step probably is not necessary to ensure that the President always turns over the reins of government when he is too ill to carry on himself. It would be far easier—and less time-consuming—to redefine the role of the President's personal physician and thereby build in some assurances that he will inform the appropriate people when his patient becomes incapacitated. . . .

A less radical and probably equally effective course was recently proposed by former Attorney General Herbert Brownell, Jr., who served under President Eisenhower: simply advise each President-elect to institute a written protocol to be followed by the White House physician, the Vice-President, and himself whenever he becomes ill. Such a protocol could set some ground rules for deciding when to temporarily assign the presidential powers and duties to the Vice-President. For example, it could specify that the President would hand over the reins for at least twenty-four hours whenever he received general anesthesia. It might also provide for mandatory meetings involving the Vice-President, the White House physician, the chief of staff, and the White House counsel before any decisions are made to have the President resume command. Ideally, each President-elect would institute such a protocol *before* being sworn into office.

In selecting a White House physician, each President should also make sure that the person meets certain qualifications—beyond those that make him a good doctor. He ought to have a thorough knowledge of the history, medical implications, and use of the Twenty-fifth Amendment. He should be familiar with the views of the American Medical Association's council on medical ethics regarding patient-doctor confidentiality and those instances in which it can be broken in the national interest. He should, in fact, be fully prepared to break his patient's confidence if it becomes necessary. And he should possess the intelligence and humility to call in outside help, when he needs it, for arriving at any judgment about presidential ability to serve. Fundamentally, the White House physician must realize that his responsibilities include not only the care of the President but also at times, the care of the nation.

The Twenty-fifth Amendment Does Not Cover Possible Disability of the Vice President

Akhil Reed Amar and Vikram David Amar

Akhil Reed Amar is a professor of law at Yale University Law School, and his brother, Vikram David Amar, is a professor of law at the University of California Hastings College of Law in San Francisco. In the following viewpoint, they explain that in the past, vice presidents have been reluctant to step in even when the president was seriously ill, because the Constitution was unclear about their status and because it might look as if they were trying to stage a coup. The Twenty-fifth Amendment fills many of the gaps, the authors say, but it leaves vital issues unaddressed. For example, if the vice president is ill or there is no vice president at a time when the president becomes ill, the provisions of the amendment will not work. Also, no provision is made for disability that occurs after a presidential election but before the inauguration. In the opinion of the Amars, Congress could fix these problems by legislation.

For a couple of hours in late June [2002], Vice President Dick Cheney became the Acting President of the United States, as George W. Bush underwent anesthesia for a scheduled medical procedure. The smooth handoff of presidential power from Bush to Cheney and back to Bush occurred pursuant to the Constitution's Twenty-fifth Amendment, which provides a detailed framework regulating various sorts of presidential disability.

Akhil Reed Amar and Vikram David Amar, "Presidency: What the 25th Amendment Overlooks," Findlaw.com, July 26, 2002. Copyright © 2002 FindLaw, a Thomson business. This column originally appeared on FindLaw.com. Reproduced by written permission.

But this Amendment did not become part of the Constitution until 1967. Why did it take Americans nearly two centuries to clarify something so important?

The unsettling answer is that both the Framers and later generations of Americans gave rather little thought to the Vice Presidency and certain specific issues involving the transfer of executive power. . . .

So long as Presidents stayed healthy in office—as did the first eight Presidents spanning the Constitution's first half century—the Vice Presidency received rather little attention.

Indeed, for much of American history—around 37 of the Constitution's first 180 years—the country did without a Vice President entirely, yet few seemed to notice. The first vacancies occurred in James Madison's Presidency, when his first term Vice President George Clinton died in 1812 and his second term Vice President Elbridge Gerry died in 1814. Under the Philadelphia Constitution, no mechanism existed to fill a Vice-Presidential vacancy—yet another signal of the low status of the office in early America.

An Acting or an Actual President?

At critical moments in American history when Presidents died or became disabled, the cracks in the Founders' Constitution became visible.

In 1841, William Henry Harrison became the first Chief Executive to die in office, and Vice President John Tyler assumed the reins of power. A nice constitutional question then arose: Was Tyler merely the Vice President *acting* as President, or did he instead actually *become* President upon Harrison's death?

The relevant constitutional text of Article II, section #1, could be read either way: "In Case of the Removal of the President from Office, or of his Death, Resignation, or Inability to discharge the Powers and Duties of the said Office, the Same shall devolve on the Vice President . . ."

Did "the Same" mean the *office* itself, or merely the *powers and duties* of the office?

If the former was the case, an ascending Vice President was entitled to the honorific title of "President." (Formal titles mattered a great deal in the old days. George Washington had wanted to be addressed as "His High Mightiness, the President of the United States and Protector of Their Liberties," but the First Congress ultimately opted for the less monarchical "Mister President.")

More importantly, if an ascending Vice President indeed became President rather than just assuming Presidential powers and duties, he could claim a President's salary, which was both higher than a Vice President's, and also immune from Congressional tampering under the rules of Article II. In turn, such immunity would enable him to wield the veto pen and other executive powers with greater independence from the legislature than would be the case if he were beholden to Congress for his very bread.

Unsurprisingly, Tyler resolved the constitutional ambiguity in his own favor, claiming that he was indeed the President, and not simply the Vice President acting as President. Following Tyler, later Vice Presidents regularly proclaimed themselves Presidents upon the deaths of their running mates, with Millard Fillmore replacing Zachary Taylor in 1850 and Andrew Johnson succeeding Abraham Lincoln in 1865.

If the President Cannot Serve

When the elected President died, and died quickly—as did Harrison, Taylor, and Lincoln—little beyond title and salary turned on whether a Vice President actually became President. But the next presidential death highlighted more troubling constitutional ambiguities. In 1881, James Garfield was shot by a dissatisfied office-seeker, then lingered for months, waxing and waning in bed. Meanwhile the nation drifted, leaderless.

Why didn't Vice President Chester A. Arthur step in, given that the President was obviously disabled? Partly because of questions raised by the Tyler precedent: If Arthur had assumed the duties of the Presidency, would he thereby *become* President under the Tyler precedent? Suppose Garfield later recovered, as for a time seemed likely. If Arthur had already become President, would Garfield be out of luck (and out of a job)? If so, Arthur would have in effect staged a coup, and permanently ousted Garfield.

Moreover, Article II section 2 neglected to specify who should decide whether Presidential "inability" existed. Garfield alone? Arthur alone? The Cabinet? The Congress? The Supreme Court?

Muddying the matter further, Garfield and Arthur came from opposite wings of the Republican Party. Garfield seemed to smile upon a professional civil service, while Arthur was a Republican "stalwart" who favored rewarding the party faithful with government jobs.

And Garfield paid dearly for his perceived views. Upon arrest, Garfield's assassin blurted out, "I did it and will go to jail for it. I am a stalwart, and Arthur will be President." In his pockets, police found a letter addressed "To the White House" proclaiming Garfield's death a "sad . . . political necessity" to "unite the Republican party," and a letter addressed to Arthur making various recommendations for Cabinet reshuffling.

Although Arthur of course had no ties to this madman, had the Vice President attempted to swoop into power, this might indeed look like a coup d'etat to America and the world.

So Arthur did nothing, and months dragged on with the country effectively without a President. Garfield eventually died, and under the Tyler precedent, Arthur then became President.

America Can Ill Afford
to Be Leaderless

A similar situation arose in 1919, when Woodrow Wilson suffered a series of strokes that left him practically incapacitated. Once again, the Vice President hung back, in part because of the uncertainty created by the Tyler and Garfield precedents. Once again, the nation endured months without an executive in charge.

But in an age of nuclear weaponry—and now, global terrorism—America can ill afford to be leaderless for long, or to have unclear rules about who is in charge. The Twenty-fifth Amendment, proposed and ratified after JFK's assassination, fills many of the gaps left open by the Founders.

For starters, the Amendment makes clear that when the President dies or resigns or is removed from office, then—and only then—the Vice President does in fact "become President." Otherwise, if the President is merely disabled (perhaps only temporarily) from exercising the powers and duties of his office, then the Vice President may step in and "assume the *powers and duties* of the office as *Acting* President" without prejudice to the President's ability to resume his post if and when he has recovered from his disability. That is exactly what [Vice President Dick] Cheney did when [George W.] Bush was under anesthesia.

The Amendment also provides a clear framework for determining whether the President is in fact disabled, and for how long. This framework specifies the precise roles of the President, the Vice President, the Cabinet, and the Congress in resolving questions about possible disability. The Amendment also authorizes Congress, by statute, to involve physicians and other experts in the disability-determination process.

Yet another provision of the Amendment allows a President, with congressional approval, to fill a Vice Presidential vacancy. Through this Amendment, Richard Nixon named Gerald Ford to the Vice Presidency when Spiro Agnew left office in 1973; and Ford in turn appointed Nelson Rockefeller in 1974 when Ford himself became President upon Nixon's resignation.

Even the Twenty-fifth Amendment, however, leaves some vital issues unaddressed. For example, it provides no satisfactory mechanism for determining *Vice-Presidential* disability. Given the health problems that many of America's Vice Presidents have historically faced—indeed, given the troubled medical history of Cheney himself—this is a serious omission.

Compounding the problem, if the Vice President ever were to be disabled (or if the Vice Presidency were at any point vacant) the Twenty-Fifth Amendment's elaborate machinery for determining *Presidential* disability will seize up; much of the key decision-making under this Amendment pivots on determinations that must be personally made by the Vice President. Also, the Amendment fails to address certain problems that arise if death or disability occurs after a presidential election but before Inauguration Day.

These flaws could probably be fixed by a simple federal statute, but thus far Congress has ignored these issues. History suggests that Americans are slow to imagine the unimaginable—even after it happens—and slower still to repair visible defects in our legal regime of presidential selection and succession.

It Is Not Clear Who Could Authorize Nuclear Weapons Use If the President and Vice President Were Unavailable

William M. Arkin

William M. Arkin is a military affairs analyst, political commentator, and journalist. In the following viewpoint he says that it is not clear who would have the authority to launch nuclear weapons if the president were disabled and the vice president were unavailable. The military's designated National Command Authorities (NCA) once consisted of the president, the secretary of defense, the Joint Chiefs of Staff, and their authorized alternates and successors. Arkin explains that the Joint Chiefs of Staff were removed from the NCA, a circumstance that is confusing because emergency action plans have given the authority to launch nuclear weapons to the president through the Joint Chiefs, omitting the secretary of defense. In addition, the Presidential Succession Act ranks the Speaker of the House and president pro tempore of the Senate ahead of the cabinet secretaries. Arkin argues that there is no explanation for the fact that, contrary to the Constitution, the definition of the NCA gives the secretary of defense what amount to presidential powers.

"As of now, I am in control here." Who doesn't remember Secretary of State Alexander Haig's mini-coup on March 30, 1981, when President Ronald Reagan was shot? That assassination attempt introduced most Americans to the intricacies of presidential succession and the military's weirdly contradictory designation of "National Command Authorities" (NCA).

William M. Arkin, "Whose Finger on the Button?" *Bulletin of the Atomic Scientists*, vol. 58, March/April, 2002, p. 73. Copyright © 2002 by the Educational Foundation for Nuclear Science, Chicago, IL 60637. Reproduced by permission of Bulletin of the Atomic Scientists: The Magazine of Global Security News & Analysis.

This year [2002], on January 11, under the direction of Defense Secretary Donald Rumsfeld, the Joint Chiefs of Staff quietly issued a new directive: "In future, please discontinue use of the term 'National Command Authorities.' Documents should instead refer specifically to the 'President' or the 'Secretary of Defense,' or both, as appropriate." In most cases, the directive adds, the term "can be replaced by the 'Secretary of Defense.'"

Is this another gaffe? Or is the nation finally safe from the Cold War contradiction that gave the defense secretary, and by extension, the uniformed military, the authority to employ nuclear weapons, regardless of the U.S. Constitution?

The Presidential Succession Act of 1947 ranked two elected officials, the speaker of the House and the president pro tempore of the Senate, after the vice president and ahead of Cabinet members. After the [President John F.] Kennedy assassination, the 25th Amendment, which addresses succession in the case of disability or inability, was adopted.

But the Kennedy administration also saw the creation of the World-Wide Military Command and Control System, which in 1962 defined the NCA as "the President, the Secretary of Defense, the Joint Chiefs of Staff, and their authorized successors and alternates." In the event of nuclear war, this system could circumvent five constitutional successors in decision-making. I say "could," because the presidential directives that govern who the "authorized successors and alternates" are have never been publicly revealed.

Over the years, the Joint Chiefs of Staff were removed as National Command Authorities. As of January [2002], Pentagon directives defined the NCA as consisting "only of the President and the Secretary of Defense or their duly deputized alternates or successors." The authority to use nuclear weapons was explicitly stated as running from the NCA to the Joint Chiefs of Staff.

Succession Unclear

There has always been confusion and contradiction, even internally, with this arrangement. The Joint Chiefs of Staff Top Secret Emergency Action Procedures for 1984, partially declassified under the Freedom of Information Act, says that "the channel of communications for execution of the SIOP [the nuclear war plan] and other time-sensitive operations shall be from the President through the Chairman [of the] Joint Chiefs of Staff to the executing commanders."

What happened to the secretary of defense? Or the Constitution? One insight comes in an account of the events of March 30, 1981 by then National Security Adviser Richard V. Allen, published in [the April 2001] *Atlantic Monthly*. An hour after the assassination attempt, White House Counsel Edwin Meese called from the hospital to reaffirm that "'the national command authority' rested with [secretary of defense] Cap Weinberger, in the absence of the Vice President."

Haig, of course, got things terribly wrong, but it is unclear what would have happened had the Soviets attacked between 2:30 that afternoon and 6:30 that evening, when Vice President George [H.W.] Bush returned to the White House from Texas.

"What if the President and Vice President are out, the Capitol has been slowed down and you can't find the Speaker or the President pro tempore of the Senate, and the Cabinet officers are all down here eating lunch?" Vice Adm. Huntington Hardisty, Director for Operations of the Joint Staff, was asked in a 1985 hearing. The admiral didn't know, and he referred Congress to the ultra-secret "continuity of government" plan and the White House Military Office.

It is now again not inconceivable to imagine Washington under attack and the succession disrupted. There are thousands of nuclear weapons on alert. We all know that [Vice President] Dick Cheney is the ultimate war-maker sitting in his bunker in Maryland. It would be nice to know why the new directive dispenses with "duly deputized alternates and successors," and gives the secretary of defense what amounts to presidential powers.

The Presidential Succession Law Would Not Be Adequate After a Catastrophic Terrorist Act

John Cornyn

John Cornyn is a Republican U.S. senator from Texas. At the time of this statement he was chairman of the Senate Subcommittee on the Constitution, Civil Rights, and Property Rights. *The following viewpoint is his opening statement at a hearing of two Senate committees that were discussing the question of presidential succession. He offers several hypothetical scenarios under which it would not be clear who was in charge if the president and vice president were both killed. If the Speaker of the House, who is next in line, were of the opposite party, the secretary of state might assert a claim to the presidency on the grounds that legislators are not "officers" and are therefore not constitutionally eligible—an opinion held by some legal scholars. In this or several other "nightmare scenarios," it would not be certain whose orders should be followed by the armed forces and law enforcement agencies, Cornyn says. He argues that it has been clear since the terrorist attack of September 11, 2001, that the presidential succession law must be quickly fixed.*

The Senate Rules Committee has jurisdiction over the Presidential succession statute. And the Senate Judiciary Committee has jurisdiction over constitutional issues, through the subcommittee I chair, the Senate Subcommittee on the Constitution, Civil Rights and Property Rights. So today's joint hearing of the two committees on the topic of Presidential succession is quite appropriate—and after 9/11, critically important. . . .

John Cornyn, testimony, joint hearing of the Senate Committee on Rules and Administration and the Senate Judiciary Committee, September 16, 2003.

[On September 9, 2003], I chaired the first in a series of hearings on continuity issues, to examine serious weaknesses in our ability to ensure continuity of the Congress. Fortunately, with respect to today's hearing, the Constitution gives us ample authority to ensure continuity of the Presidency— even as it may be inadequate with respect to Congress itself. Unfortunately, however, the current Presidential succession law, enacted in 1947, has long troubled the nation's top legal scholars across the political spectrum as both unconstitutional and unworkable.

A Dangerous Situation

This situation is dangerous and intolerable. We must have a system in place, so that it is always clear—and beyond all doubt—who the President is, especially in times of national crisis. Yet our current succession law badly fails that standard. Imagine the following scenarios:

The President and Vice President are both killed. Under current law, next in line to act as President is the Speaker of the House. Suppose, however, that the Speaker is a member of the party opposite the now-deceased President, and that the Secretary of State, acting out of party loyalty, asserts a competing claim to the Presidency. The Secretary argues that members of Congress are legislators and, thus, are not "officer[s]" who are constitutionally eligible to act as President. Believe it or not, the Secretary has a strong case—in fact, he can cite for support the views of James Madison, the father of our Constitution, who argued this very point in 1792, as well as legal scholars on the left and right. Who is the President? Whose orders should be followed by our armed forces, by our intelligence agencies, and by our domestic law enforcement bureaus? If lawsuits are filed, will courts take the case? How long will they take to rule, how will they rule and will their rulings be respected?

Senator John Cornyn, here being administered the oath of office by then-vice president Dick Cheney, contends that the Twenty-fifth Amendment does not clearly dictate who would assume leadership if both the president and vice president were killed. AP Images.

Or imagine that, once again, the President and Vice President are killed, and the Speaker is a member of the opposite party. This time, however, the Speaker declines the opportunity to act as President—in a public-minded effort to prevent a change in party control of the White House as the result of a terrorist attack. And imagine that the President pro tempore of the Senate acts similarly. The Secretary of State thus becomes Acting President. In subsequent weeks, however, the Secretary takes a series of actions that upset the Speaker. The Speaker responds by asserting his right under the statute to take over as Acting President. The Secretary counters that he cannot constitutionally be removed from the White House by anyone other than a President or Vice President, because under the Constitution, he is entitled to act as President "until the disability [of the President or Vice President] be removed, or a President shall be elected." Confusion and litigation ensue. Who is the President?

Or imagine that the President, Vice President, and Speaker are all killed, along with numerous members of Congress—for example as the result of an attack during the State of the Union address. The remaining members of the House—a small fraction of the entire membership, representing just a narrow geographic region of the country and a narrow portion of the ideological spectrum—claim that they can constitute a quorum, and then attempt to elect a new Speaker. That new Speaker then argues that he is Acting President. The Senate President pro tempore and the Secretary of State each assert competing claims that they are President. Who is the President?

Or finally, notice that the President, Vice President, Speaker, Senate President pro tempore, and the members of the Cabinet all live and work in the greater Washington, D.C. area. Now, imagine how easy it would be for a catastrophic terrorist attack on Washington to kill or incapacitate the entire line of succession to the Presidency, as well as the President himself. Who is the President?

Nightmare Scenarios

In every one of these scenarios, we do not know for sure who the President is—a chilling thought for all Americans. In an age of terrorism and a time of war, this is no longer mere fodder for Tom Clancy novels and episodes of "The West Wing." These nightmare scenarios are serious concerns after 9/11. On that terrible day, federal officers ordered a dramatic evacuation of the White House, even shouting at White House staffers: "Run!" On that day, the Secret Service executed its emergency plan to protect and defend the line of Presidential succession—for the first time ever in American history, according to some reports. And in subsequent months, the President and Vice President were constantly kept separate, for months and months after 9/11, precisely out of the fear that continuity of the Presidency might otherwise be in serious jeopardy.

We must fix the Presidential succession law—and fix it now—so that these nightmare scenarios will never come true, and will never again be able to haunt the American people. . . . After all, we have had two years since 9/11 to do this. Two years is too long, and the time to plan for the unthinkable is now.

Under the Twenty-fifth Amendment a President Could Be Supplanted for Political Reasons

Adam R.F. Gustafson

In the following viewpoint, written when he was a student at Yale Law School, Adam R.F. Gustafson argues that the phrase "unable to discharge" in reference to the president's duties has different meanings in Sections 3 and 4 of the Twenty-fifth Amendment and that the fact that this has not been recognized could lead to trouble. The circumstances under which the president should voluntarily transfer his power to the vice president under Section 3 are different from those in which it should be taken away from him under Section 4. For example, it should not be possible for the vice president to invoke Section 4 when the president undergoes minor surgery, but some scholars argue that if "unable" means the same thing in both places, he could. On the other hand, presidents may be reluctant to use Section 3 when it is desirable, for fear of setting a precedent that could carry over to Section 4. The congressional review required by Section 4 is not enough to protect a president from being ousted, says Gustafson. Among other reasons, the vice president could take control and pursue his or her own agenda under Section 4 before Congress was consulted and would have days to consolidate power.

At the Constitutional Convention in 1787, Delegate John Dickinson of Delaware raised a question that, in [James] Madison's notes at least, met with an uncomfortable silence: "What is the extent of the term 'disability' & who is to be the

Adam R.F. Gustafson, "Presidential Inability and Subjective Meaning," *Yale Law & Policy Review*, vol. 27, 2009, pp. 459–470. Copyright 2009 Yale Law & Policy Review. Reproduced by permission.

judge of it?" He was referring to what became the presidential succession clause in Article II. Debate on this provision was immediately postponed, and Dickinson's prescient question went unanswered for almost two centuries. In 1967 a new generation of constitutional authors answered the second part of his query in the Twenty-Fifth Amendment, providing procedures whereby the President may be the judge of his own inability or, in the event he is unable or unwilling so to declare, the Vice President and Cabinet may declare him unable with Congress as the court of appeal.

The first part of Dickinson's question—the definition of presidential inability—has never been directly and authoritatively answered. Regardless of who is judging presidential inability—the President himself or his Vice President and Cabinet—the textual precondition is identical, and identically vague. The question in each instance is whether the President is "unable to discharge the powers and duties of his office." On the textual surface, the only difference between the inability provisions of these sections lies in the actor or actors who determine presidential inability. The Constitution offers no explicit guidance for evaluating presidential ability—no measure of physical vigor, mental acuity, or emotional stability— but only provides two sets of constitutional actors and procedures whereby that evaluation may be made. The framers of the Twenty-Fifth Amendment intentionally declined to provide a clear constitutional rule in response to Dickinson's first question, but the structure and context of the Amendment they crafted and the legislative history they wrote in the process suggest two separate categories of presidential inability.

Previous expositors of the "unable to discharge" phrase have erroneously assumed that it has the same meaning whether invoked by the President or his subordinates. In spite of the traditional presumption that identical phrases have the same meaning, a careful reading of the presidential inability clauses of the Twenty-Fifth Amendment, informed by constitutional structure and confirmed by legislative and application history, demands two different constructions of the identical "unable to discharge" phrases. The President enjoys absolute discretion in his construction of the inability provision of Section 3: Structure demands and history confirms that as long as the President is able to make a rational decision to temporarily yield the powers of his office to the Vice President, he may do so no matter what underlying condition or circumstance provokes that action. Section 4 by contrast demands a much narrower construction of its inability provision by the Vice President and Cabinet: Section 4 is only available when the President is so severely impaired that he is unable to make or communicate a rational decision to step down temporarily of his own accord. . . .

The Presidency in Jeopardy

The present state of scholarly opinion on the meaning of Sections 3 and 4 of the Twenty-Fifth Amendment endangers the presidency by its simplistic understanding of presidential inability. Because the "unable to discharge" phrase has the same semantic content in each section, its interpreters have assumed that the phrase is univocal—that it admits of only one legal meaning. If this were so, any legitimate construction of presidential inability in one section could apply to the other, and the history of presidential applications of Section 3 for minor, short-term impairments would create dangerous precedent that an ambitious Vice President and misguided Cabinet could use to oust the President under Section 4 for a critical period, or even permanently with the cooperation of Congress.

The mistaken notion that the "unable to discharge" phrases in Sections 3 and 4 must be subject to the same construction has existed from the beginning. The Amendment's opponents in Congress warned that Section 4 would transfer too much executive power to the Vice President and Cabinet, risking a coup d'état in the White House. Even proponents of the Amendment failed to explicitly distinguish between the "unable to discharge" phrases in Sections 3 and 4, although their section-specific definitions and hypothetical applications confirm that different constructions must apply in each section. Instead the Amendment's sponsors defended Section 4 with reference to the history of deferential Vice Presidents.

Neither of the two major scholarly commissions on the Amendment suggested distinct constructions of the two "unable to discharge" phrases. The 1988 Miller Center Commission on Presidential Disability and the Twenty-Fifth Amendment advised routine use of Section 3 for even "borderline cases" of transitory inability, and restraint in application of Section 4; however, the Commission never offered a constitutional justification for this distinction or suggested that the Vice President and Cabinet are actually more limited in their construction of "unable to discharge" than the President is. The Commission dismissed the concern that liberal use of Section 3 by the President would encourage power grabs by broadening the definition of presidential inability in Section 4: "[T]he fear of a coup by a vice president is based on a false analogy with other political systems. Historically the defects of the American vice presidency have not been the temptation to seize power but the refusal to accept power inherent in the office." However, the historical examples of vice presidential modesty the Commission cites occurred before the Twenty-Fifth Amendment, and each Vice President had his own context-dependent reason for restraint. Moreover, the office of the Vice President has acquired considerable political power since Vice President [Thomas] Marshall allowed the First Lady to govern in sick President [Woodrow] Wilson's stead. Indeed, the rate of expansion of Vice Presidential power has increased because of the passage of the Twenty-Fifth Amendment. The Miller Center Commission ignored this evolving power dynamic. The proposals of the 1995 Working Group on Presidential Disability also failed to articulate a difference between legitimate constructions of Sections 3 and 4, though they did distinguish impairment (a medical judgment) from presidential inability (a political judgment). A Subcommittee on Disability and Impairment listed "[c]onditions invariably producing complete incapacitation" that should trigger automatic consideration of either Section 3 or Section 4, but did not distinguish between the types of inability proper to each section.

Two Standards

Many scholars independently have proposed guidelines for diagnosing presidential inability, but none has suggested that the "unable to discharge" phrase is subject to different constructions in Sections 3 and 4. Instead they have struggled to give it a single meaning that makes sense in both sections. Because they equate the two standards, some proposals would allow the Vice President to invoke Section 4 in circumstances where the legislative history of the Amendment expressly rejects its application, and which are inconsistent with constitutional structure. Herbert Abrams opines that "Section 4 may be utilized" any time the president fails to invoke Section 3 before undergoing general anesthesia, even for "[p]lanned, minor surgical procedures." He also would allow the Vice President and Cabinet to oust a terminally ill President who was not otherwise incapacitated. Both possibilities contradict the legislative history and structure of the amendment, but follow naturally from a univocal construction of the "unable to discharge" phrases: If a President may declare himself "unable" under Section 3 for a colonoscopy, and if that phrase has the same meaning in both sections, then the Vice President and Cabinet may declare the President "unable" during the same procedure under Section 4.

Other scholars, starting from the same mistaken presumption of univocality but wary of endangering the presidency, would apply the strict standard for inability under Section 4 to both sections. These scholars caution against liberal use of Section 3 by the President for fear that such applications would create dangerous precedent for declaring inability under Section 4. In an article advocating this watered-down approach to Section 3, Scott Gant states the univocal presumption explicitly:

> [T]he inability provisions of Sections 3 and 4 have the same meaning as one another.... [I]t seems apparent that circumstances enabling a President to invoke Section 3 would also permit the Vice President and the cabinet to employ Section 4. After all, the two provisions use identical language to describe the condition prompting the transfer of power from the President to the Vice President.

Imposing the narrow standard of Section 4 inability upon the President's discretionary Section 3 power, however, may be as damaging as the reverse alternative. Just such a misunderstanding of the meaning of Section 3 inability led, President [Ronald] Reagan to disclaim its application to "brief and temporary periods of incapacity" instead of explicitly invoking it at the first occasion. This approach undermines the purpose of Section 3—to promote continuity in the executive branch by encouraging the President to declare temporary inability even for short periods. By failing to approach presidential inability with a nuanced theory of constitutional construction, each of these scholars has promoted either unhealthy avoidance of Section 3 or cavalier exploitation of Section 4.

Congressional Review Inadequate

Some scholars protest that even if the Vice President and Cabinet were to import a broad construction of "unable to discharge" from Section 3 into Section 4, the congressional check built into Section 4 would prevent any mischief. This theory assumes incorrectly that since more members of Congress are needed to affirm a President's suspension under Section 4 than to impeach and convict him under Article II, Section 5, the Twenty-Fifth Amendment is necessarily more protective of presidential power than the impeachment process is. While it is true that the double supermajority requirement of Section 4 is more protective of the President than the Article II impeachment and conviction process, which requires only a majority of the House of Representatives, this procedural hurdle is only one of several factors that make Section 4 different from impeachment. The double supermajority requirement does not eliminate the risk created by a singular construction of the "unable to discharge" phrases.

First, the Twenty-Fifth Amendment and Article II impeachment exist to remedy different presidential defects, so not every President separated from his powers by Section 4 could also be impeached and convicted. Unlike in an impeachment proceeding, Congress would not have to find the President guilty of wrongdoing to find him "unable to discharge the powers and duties of his office." Thus, if the Vice President, Cabinet, and Congress equate Section 4 inability with the flexible standard of Section 3, an unpopular President who has committed no crime is at greater risk of Congressional removal under the Twenty-Fifth Amendment than Article II impeachment, in spite of the double supermajority required by the former.

Second, Congress may be more likely to affirm the President's inability under the Twenty-Fifth Amendment than to impeach him under Article II because a finding of Section 4 inability is not necessarily permanent. While removal by impeachment is final, the President may appeal a declaration of Section 4 inability an unlimited number of times. This difference may make inability seem to Congress less severe than impeachment. The difference may be illusory, however, because Congress is unlikely to reinstate a President whom the Executive and Legislative branches have already declared incapable of serving in that office.

Third, the damage of an improper declaration of inability under Section 4 is immediate. Unlike removal by impeachment and conviction, which takes effect only after both Houses of Congress have voted against the President, removal by Section 4 of the Twenty-Fifth Amendment occurs before Congress even enters the scene. Congress only votes on the President's inability after the Vice President has already become Acting President, the President has transmitted "his written declaration that no inability exists," *and* the Vice President and Cabinet have transmitted a second declaration to the contrary. Moreover, the Vice President and Cabinet are allowed four days from the time of the President's appeal to decide whether to transmit their second declaration. Thus, the Acting President can enjoy at least four days of presidential power—four days to advance his own policy goals, to prove himself as a capable executive, and to acclimate Congress and the public to his presence in the Oval Office. By the time Congress is allowed to vote, the deck may already be stacked against the President: The appellate posture of the case before Congress, doubts cast on the President's ability, popular interim leadership by the Acting President, and reluctance to upset the status quo again, would all work in the Vice President's favor.

Finally, even if Congressional action or inaction ultimately restores the President to his office, the four-day period—up to twenty-seven days if Congress is slow to assemble and cannot reach a decision—may be enough for the Acting President to accomplish whatever goals led him to challenge the President's ability in the first place. Thus, the existence of legislative review is an insufficient protection against the risks of a univocal interpretation of presidential inability in Sections 3 and 4. . . .

The prevailing confusion about how to construe the Twenty-Fifth Amendment's inability provisions can be remedied if Congress and the Executive branch commit themselves to detaching their construction of Section 4 from the President's more expansive construction of Section 3. By coming to grips with this unusual contravention of the intratextualist presumption, both purposes of the Twenty-Fifth Amendment will be advanced: The President will be encouraged to transfer power to the Vice President any time his ability to govern may be diminished, and the President will act without fear that his voluntary invocation of the Amendment will be used against him or his successors. Continued equivocation endangers the oval office. [As Representative Emanuel Celler stated in Congress:] "Let us stop playing Presidential inability roulette."

Solutions to Potential Problems of Presidential Succession and Disability

Congressional Leaders May Not Belong in the Line of Succession to the Presidency

Thomas H. Neale

Thomas H. Neale is a specialist in American national government for the Congressional Research Service. In the following portion of a report on presidential succession that he prepared for Congress, he explains that it is not clear what the Constitution means by the word "officer" when it grants Congress the power to establish the presidential line of succession. Some scholars, he says, believe that the Speaker of the House and the president pro tempore of the Senate are not constitutionally eligible because they are merely officers of Congress, not officers of the government in the sense the Constitution means. Under this interpretation, the presidential succession acts of 1792 and 1947 are unconstitutional. Congressional leaders were included by these acts under the democratic principle that they are elected to their positions, unlike members of the Cabinet, who are appointed. However, critics of this reasoning point out that they are elected by the voters of only their own district or state. Some also argue that a person acting as president should be of the same political party as the person who was elected, which may not be the case with members of Congress. Still another problem with including congressional leaders, Neale says, is that they must resign their previous positions to become acting president, which they may be reluctant to do.

The events of September 11, 2001 and the prospect of a "decapitation" of the U.S. government by an act of mass terrorism have led to a reexamination of many previously

Thomas H. Neale, "Contemporary Analysis: Presidential Succession in the Post-9/11 Era," Presidential Succession: Perspectives, Contemporary Analysis, and 110th Congress Proposed Legislation, October 3, 2008. Reproduced by permission.

long-settled elements of presidential succession and continuity of government on the federal level. A number of proposals to revise the Succession Act of 1947 have been introduced in the 108th through 110th Congresses. Some of these were in the nature of "housekeeping" legislation; that is, they proposed to insert the office of Secretary of the Department of Homeland Security into the line of succession, as has been done in the past when new cabinet departments are created by Congress. Others proposed more complex changes in the legislation. . . .

Several issues dominate current discussions over revising the order of presidential succession. Some are "hardy perennials," constitutional questions that have risen in every debate on succession law. . . . Others reflect more recent concerns.

Defining the Term "Officer"

Do the Speaker and the President pro tempore qualify as "Officers" for the purposes of presidential succession? There is no question as to Congress's constitutional ability to provide for presidential succession. This power is directly granted by Article II, Section 1, clause 6, modified by the 25th Amendment. . . . What is in question here is what the Constitution means by the word "Officer." The interpretation of this phrase, and, by extension, whether the Speaker and President pro-tempore are constitutionally eligible to succeed the President has been perhaps the most durable element in the succession debate over time. Are they "officers" in the sense as noted in Article II, or are their positions as *officers of the Congress*, established in Article I, Sections 2 and 3, so fundamentally different that they are ineligible to succeed. The succession acts of both 1792 and 1947 assumed that the language was sufficiently broad as to include officers of Congress, the President pro tempore of the Senate and the Speaker of the House of Representatives (the 1792 act specified this order of succession; the 1947 act reversed the order, placing the Speaker of the House first in line, followed by the President pro tempore).

Some observers assert that these two congressional officials are *not* officers in the sense intended by the Constitution, and that the 1792 act was, and the 1947 act is, constitutionally questionable. . . .

This point was raised in congressional debate over both the Succession Act of 1792 and that of 1947. In the former case, opinion appears to have been divided: James Madison (arguably the single most formative influence on the Constitution, and a serving Representative when the 1792 act was debated) held that officers of Congress were not eligible to succeed. Other Representatives who had also served as delegates to the Constitutional Convention were convinced to the contrary. In addition, political issues also contributed to the debate in 1792. Fordham University Law School Dean and succession scholar John D. Feerick notes that the Federalist-dominated Senate insisted on inclusion of the President pro tempore and the Speaker. He cites contemporary sources that the Senate sought to exclude the Secretary of State largely because the incumbent was Thomas Jefferson, who was locked in a bitter dispute with Alexander Hamilton and his Federalist supporters. Jefferson was the acknowledged leader of the Anti-Federalists, the group that later emerged as the Jeffersonian Republican, or Democratic Republican, Party. It thus may be inferred that the provisions of the Succession Act of 1792 may have been the result of political machinations and personal animosities.

Questions as to the constitutional legitimacy of the Speaker and the President pro tempore as potential successors to the President and Vice President recurred during debate on the 1947 succession act. . . .

Given the diversity of opinion on this question, and the continuing relevance of historical practice and debate, the issue of constitutional legitimacy remains an important element of any congressional effort to amend or replace the Succession Act of 1947.

A second category of succession issues includes political questions and administrative concerns.

The Political Aspect

These two interrelated issues collectively comprise what might be termed the political aspect of presidential succession. Democratic principle was perhaps the dominant factor contributing to the passage of the 1947 succession act. Simply stated, it is the assertion that presidential and vice presidential succession should be settled first on popularly elected officials, rather than the appointed members of the Cabinet, as was the case under the 1886 act. According to Feerick, the 1886 act's provisions aroused criticism not long after Vice President Harry Truman became President on the death of Franklin D. Roosevelt. President Truman responded less than two months after succeeding to the presidency, when he proposed to Congress the revisions to succession procedures that, when amended, eventually were enacted as the Succession Act of 1947. . . .

Conversely, critics of this reasoning assert that the Speaker, while chosen by a majority of his peers in the House, has won approval by the *voters* only in his own congressional district. Further, although elected by the voters in his home state, the President pro tempore of the Senate serves as such by virtue of being the longest-serving Senator of the majority party.

Against the case for democratic succession urged by President Truman, the value of party continuity, best assured by having a cabinet officer in the first place of succession, is asserted by some observers. The argument here is that a person acting as President under these circumstances should be of the same political party as the previous incumbent, in order to assure continuity of the political affiliation, and, presumably, the policies of the candidate chosen by the voters in the last election. According to this reasoning, succession by a Speaker or President pro tempore of a different party would be a reversal of the people's mandate that would be inherently undemocratic. Moreover, they note, this possibility is not remote: since passage of the Succession Act of 1947, the nation has experienced "divided government," that is, control of the presidency by one party and either or both houses of Congress by another, for 36 of the 61 intervening years. As Yale University Professor Akhil Amar noted in his testimony at the 2003 joint Senate committee hearing, ". . . [the current succession provisions] can upend the results of a Presidential election. If Americans elect party A to the White House, why should we end up with party B?" . . .

Efficient Conduct of the Presidency

Some observers also question the potential effect on conduct of the presidency if the Speaker or President pro tempore were to succeed to the office. Would these persons, whose duties and experience are essentially legislative, have the skills necessary to serve as chief executive? Moreover, it is noted that these offices have often been held by persons in late middle age, or even old age, whose health and energy levels might be limited. As Miller Baker noted in his testimony before the 2003 joint committee hearings, ". . . history shows that senior cabinet officers such as the Secretary of State and the Secretary of Defense are generally more likely to be better suited to the exercise of presidential duties than legislative officers. The President pro tempore, traditionally the senior member of the party in control of the Senate, may be particularly ill-suited to the exercise of presidential duties due to reasons of health and age." Conversely, it can be noted that the Speaker, particularly, has extensive executive duties, both as presiding officer of the House, and as de facto head of the extensive structure of committees, staff, and enabling infrastructure that comprises the larger entity of the House of Representatives. . . .

"Bumping"

This question centers on the 1947 Succession Act provision that officers acting as President under the act do so only until the disability or failure to qualify of any officer higher in the order of succession is removed. If the disability is removed, the previously entitled officer can supplant ("bump") the person then acting as President. For instance, assuming the death, disability, or failure to qualify of the President, the Vice President, the Speaker, the President pro tempore, or a senior cabinet secretary is acting as President. Supplantion could take place under any one of several scenarios. . . .

Critics assert that the supplantation provisions could lead to dangerous instability in the presidency during a time of national crisis. For example, [Howard Wasserman] testified as follows:

> Imagine a catastrophic attack kills the president, vice-president and congressional leadership. The secretary of state assumes the duties of the presidency. But whenever Congress elects a new Speaker or president pro tem, that new leader may 'bump' the secretary of state. The result would be three presidents within a short span of time.

Moreover, as noted previously, any person who becomes acting President must resign his previous position, in the case of the Speaker and President pro tempore, or have his appointment vacated by the act of oath taking. It is certainly foreseeable that public officials might hesitate to forfeit their offices and end their careers before taking on the acting presidency, particularly if the prospect of supplantation loomed. The "bumping" question has been used by critics of legislative succession as an additional argument for removing the Speaker and President pro tempore from the line of succession. Another suggested remedy would be to amend the Succession Act of 1947 to eliminate the right of "prior entitled" individuals to supplant an acting President who is acting due to a vacancy in the office of President and Vice President. Relatedly, other proposals would amend the law to permit cabinet officials to take a leave of absence from their departments while serving as acting President in cases of presidential and vice presidential disability. They could thus return to their prior duties on recovery of either the President and Vice President, and their services would not be lost to the nation, nor would there be the need to nominate and confirm a replacement.

Recommended Changes to the Line of Succession to the Presidency

Continuity of Government Commission

The Continuity of Government Commission, a project of the American Enterprise Institute (AEI) and the Brookings Institution, two Washington, D.C., think tanks, was created to study and recommend reforms to ensure the continuity of the nation's governmental institutions in the event of a catastrophic attack. The following viewpoint consists of its recommendations for changes in the line of succession to the presidency. First, the report recommends adding federal officials who live outside Washington, D.C., to the line of succession. Among its other recommendations are removing congressional leaders from the succession, reordering the line of succession to put the most qualified cabinet officers first, and establishing procedures to secure the line of succession during the period before the inauguration of an incoming president.

Given the possibility of an attack with weapons of mass destruction, it is essential that the line of Presidential succession include at least some individuals who live and work outside of the Washington, D.C. area.

There are several ways to achieve this objective. For instance, federal officials such as ambassadors and governors, perhaps in the order of the size of their state or the creation of the states, could be included in the line of succession as a

Preserving Our Institutions: The Continuity of The Presidency: The Second Report of the Continuity of Government Commission, Washington, DC: Continuity of Government Commission, 2009. Copyright © 2009 by the American Enterprise Institute. All rights reserved. Reproduced by permission.

last resort. The Commission's preferred solution, however, is to create four or five new federal offices. The President would appoint important figures to these offices, and they would be confirmed by the Senate. The Commission envisions these individuals would largely be former high government officials that the President felt comfortable appointing such as former presidents, former secretaries of state, former members of Congress, or even sitting governors all located outside of Washington, D.C. Though the Constitution prevents presidents from seeking third terms in office, former presidents are, indeed, eligible to be selected in the Presidential line of succession. Some states prohibit state officeholders from holding federal office, but other states allow it. Sitting governors from the states that allow dual office-holding could also be considered by the President and the Senate. These new offices would sit at the end of the line of succession as a failsafe if a catastrophic attack on Washington wiped out others in the line of succession.

The Commission also recommends that only the top four cabinet members be included in the line of succession, with the officers outside of Washington as last in the line of succession instead of the lower profile cabinet members under the current law.

It is important to keep these new officers informed of matters that would be relevant if they were suddenly thrust into the presidency following a catastrophic attack. Lower profile cabinet members are not as a matter of course briefed regularly and thoroughly on national security matters. However, these newly created officers would presumably have high levels of past experience that would help them in the position of President. But in addition, the White House should strive to include these officers in regular (at least monthly) national security briefings, as a part of their duties as Officers of the United States.

Vice Presidential Vacancies

Vice President	Period For Which Elected	Termination of Service	Reason for Termination
George Clinton	March 4, 1809–1813	April 20, 1812	Death
Elbridge Gerry	March 4, 1813–1817	November 23, 1814	Death
John C. Calhoun	March 4, 1829–1833	December 28, 1832	Resignation
John Tyler	March 4, 1841–1845	April 4, 1841	Succession
Millard Fillmore	March 4, 1849–1853	July 9, 1850	Succession
William R. King	March 4, 1853–1857	April 18, 1853	Death
Andrew Johnson	March 4, 1865–1869	April 15, 1865	Succession
Henry Wilson	March 4, 1873–1877	November 22, 1875	Death
Chester A. Arthur	March 4, 1881–1885	September 19, 1881	Succession
Thomas A. Hendricks	March 4, 1885–1889	November 25, 1885	Death
Garret A. Hobart	March 4, 1897–1901	November 21, 1889	Death
Theodore Roosevelt	March 4, 1901–1905	September 14, 1901	Succession
James S. Sherman	March 4, 1909–1913	October 30, 1912	Death
Calvin Coolidge	March 4, 1921–1925	August 2, 1923	Succession
Harry S. Truman	January 20, 1945–1949	April 12, 1945	Succession
Lyndon B. Johnson	January 20, 1961–1965	November 22, 1963	Succession
*Spiro Agnew	January 20, 1969–1977	October 10, 1973	Resignation
*Gerald Ford	October 12, 1973–January 20, 1977	August 9, 1974	Succession

*Gerald Ford was never elected. He assumed the presidency upon Richard Nixon's resignation. There was an additional 2 day vacancy between Spiro Agnew's resignation and Gerald Ford's assumption of the powers of the Vice Presidency on October 12, 1973.

TAKEN FROM: Continuity of Government Commission, *Preserving Our Institutions: Presidential Succession.* Washington, DC: A E I-Brookings, June 2009.

Remove Congressional Leaders

There is reason to believe that including congressional leaders in the line of succession may be unconstitutional. If a Congressional leader not from the President's party were to assume the presidency, it could lead to a destabilizing change of party for the federal government. Additionally, . . . the inclusion of Congressional leaders could lead to multiple successors in a short period of time. American constitutional structure makes the most sense if Article I gives Congress the power to specify which *executive* branch figures should be in the line of succession.

[President] Harry Truman felt that successors should be elected officials and that a president should not be able to appoint his own successors. While it is true that Congressional leaders are elected, they are elected only by their state or district. The election criterion, powerful as it is, is simply not compelling enough to outweigh the drawbacks, constitutional and otherwise, from having congressional leaders in the line. For reasons of stability, it is preferable that a president select successors who are sympathetic to the party or standing agenda of the White House and that the selection not be made just by the President, but also with the advice and consent of the Senate.

Excluding Congressional leaders would eliminate the possibility that the presidency would shift to the other party if a catastrophic attack killed both the President and Vice President. It would eliminate the possibility of a rump group of a handful of lawmakers choosing a Speaker of the House who would then become president. It would also eliminate the provision in the current law whereby a subsequently elected Speaker bumps out a cabinet member who has taken over for the President. This provision could lead to three presidents in a short period of time.

Finally, the exclusion of Congressional leaders would improve succession during incapacitation. If the presidency must

pass to a Congressional leader because of a temporary incapacitation, then it would be very difficult for Congressional
leaders to step in for the President. Unless the Congressional
leaders were willing to resign their congressional seats, they
could not take over the presidency. And once they resigned,
they could not reclaim their seats unless they ran for the seat
and won in the next scheduled election.

The commission recognizes the political difficulty of removing Congressional leaders from the line of succession.
Short of excluding the Congressional leaders altogether, . . .
smaller steps might be taken. First, Congress should remove
the "bumping procedure," by which a subsequent Speaker
could claim the presidency from a cabinet successor. Instead,
the law should allow a living Speaker or Senate leader to take
the presidency if the President and Vice President are killed,
but if the Speaker and Senate leader are also killed, then the
Cabinet member who becomes president should remain president for the remainder of the term, as the Constitution prescribes, and as would increase the legitimacy of the succession
in the eyes of the American people. . . .

Short of removing the leaders, Congress should change the
line of succession so that the congressional leaders will only
be in the line of succession for the death of a president, but
not for the incapacitation, a scenario in which their assumption would cause much confusion. Congress could also choose
to prevent congressional leaders from taking charge in the
case of impeachment of the President, a situation in which
some leaders might stand to gain. . . .

Congress would face its own formidable problems in the
event of an attack that killed a large number of its members.
In this context, the reconstitution of Congress is also important because the congressional leaders chosen after the attack
might succeed the presidency. Congress should allow the appointment of temporary officials to fill vacancies in the House
of Representatives so that Congress can continue functioning

after an attack. Also, the House should clarify the processes through which vacancies in the speakership are filled, keeping in mind that a new speaker could automatically assume the presidency. If the speakership were to automatically devolve onto minor members of the House, America could see a relatively insignificant political figure elevated to the presidency. The House should ensure that no individual will assume the presidency without a vote in the full House of Representatives, not by fiat or by the vote of an unrepresentative handful of surviving lawmakers.

Special Election for President

The Constitution allows for a special presidential election if the President and the Vice President are killed. Similarly, the first Presidential Succession Act allowed for such an election. But subsequent succession acts have not included such a provision. Congress should reform our current law to provide for a special election within five months if a simultaneous vacancy of the presidency and vice presidency occurs in the first two years of a presidential term. Were such an election not to occur, the interim successor should serve until the end of the term.

Reorder the Line of Succession

The order of the line of succession should be reconsidered. Since the line of succession was established by the 1947 Presidential Succession Act, the only changes have been to add the secretaries of the newly created departments to the end of the line. In fact, all of the Cabinet officers are arranged in the order of the creation of their departments. While the chronology of the creation of the departments might be a rough guide to their relative importance, Congress should not follow this formula blindly. It should think again from scratch what the best order of succession is, especially considering the emergence of the real possibility of a catastrophic attack on Washington.

The "Big Four" departments should then be examined and reordered to best address a catastrophic attack. It is unlikely that both the President and the Vice President would die simultaneously except in the event of an outside attack. The commission therefore recommends that the order of succession start with the Secretary of State to be followed by the Secretary of Defense, Attorney General and the Secretary of Treasury.

The commission also recommends that the lower profile cabinet members be replaced by the offices created for figures outside of Washington. The lower profile cabinet officials are often picked for their expertise in a particular policy area, are less well known than the "Big Four" cabinet members, and are less intimately involved in matters of national security that would be paramount at the time of an attack.

Remove Acting Secretaries

The Second Presidential Succession Act (in place from 1877 to 1947) explicitly stated that only department heads confirmed by the Senate for the position of department head were in the line of succession. The current act, however, can easily cause confusion as it allows for acting secretaries who were confirmed by the Senate for lower level posts to be in the line of succession. The current line of succession is also particularly ambiguous around the inauguration when a number of departments are briefly headed by acting secretaries pending the confirmation of cabinet secretaries in the new administration.

Clarify Procedures

A catastrophic attack may involve serious injury to the President and the deaths of others in the line of succession. While procedures for a vice president taking over for an incapacitated president are well laid out by the 25th Amendment, procedures for succession by lower officials are not. Congress has the authority to legally prescribe the exact procedure for a lesser cabinet official taking over for an incapacitated president. The law probably could not require the lower level official to obtain the consent of other cabinet members, as this is a constitutional provision of the 25th Amendment provided for the Vice President. But it could provide guidance as to how the transfer might take place and how Congress is to be notified.

Further, Congress should clarify what would happen if a majority of the cabinet were unavailable for the Vice President to consult with when a president is incapacitated. Under a provision of the 25th Amendment, Congress could specify an alternative body with which the Vice President could consult and obtain a majority in order to take over the presidency. For example, Congress could indicate that in case the Vice President is unable to secure a majority of the cabinet due to death or incapacity, the Vice President shall secure a majority of governors or another body outside of Washington.

Fix Inaugural Scenarios

Congress and the political parties should take preventative measures to secure the line of succession in the very dangerous times both during and before the inauguration. Congress must not allow a gap of even several hours during which the line of succession for an incoming president has not yet been established and the outgoing president's cabinet has resigned.

This could be accomplished simply through cooperation between the outgoing president and the incoming president— representing a mere change in custom, rather than a change in law. The outgoing president could submit the names of several of the incoming president's cabinet nominees to the Senate and the Senate could then convene and confirm these nominees on the day before the inauguration or the morning of January 20th. This way there would be an established line of succession at the inaugural ceremony. Additionally, several members of the line might be sent out of town for the ceremony. If recommendation #1, the appointment of officers in the line of succession who would live outside of Washington, were adopted, the Senate could also confirm these figures before the inauguration, as the congressional hearings presumably would have been completed in early January.

The commission also recommends shortening as much as possible the period between the casting of electoral votes and their counting by Congress. These dates are relics of an earlier era when communications were slower and less reliable than they are today. Congress should move the date on which the electors meet to cast their votes closer to January 6th, leaving at most a gap of one or two days. This interim period breeds confusion because there is no formal president-elect, even though the electors' choices are now obvious.

Finally, political parties should plan for the possibility of the death of their president-elect and vice president-elect. They should reexamine their procedures for selecting a new nominee to send to the electors in the event of the death of a nominee. Such procedures should be designed so as to make the selection of nominees as broadly acceptable as possible to prepare for the extreme possibility that both nominees are killed.

The Line of Succession to the Presidency Should Include People Based Outside Washington

M. Miller Baker

M. Miller Baker is an attorney who has served in the Justice Department and as counsel to the Senate Judiciary Committee. His focus is on constitutional litigation, and he has appeared on television news programs in connection with constitutional matters. *The following viewpoint is a portion of his testimony before a congressional committee that was studying presidential succession. He points out that the events of September 11, 2001, could have been even worse if the terrorists' objective had been to decapitate the U.S. government. If the White House and Capitol had been struck, most of the people in the line of succession would have been eliminated. Furthermore, as long as congressional leaders who may be of a different party from the president are in the line of succession, terrorists could intentionally undo the results of the last U.S. election. In any case, Baker argues, these leaders may not be qualified to assume presidential duties because of age and poor health. Some of the cabinet officers may not be qualified either, as they are not chosen for presidential attributes. In Baker's opinion the law should be changed to reorder the line of succession, and in the long run, there should be a constitutional amendment to allow the inclusion of successors who are not officers of the United States, so that people who live outside Washington, D.C., can be included.*

M. Miller Baker, "Testimony: Ensuring the Continuity of the Presidency," Joint Hearing before the Committee on Rules and Administration and the Committee on the Judiciary United States Senate, September 16, 2003. Reproduced by permission of the author.

The terrorist attack on America on September 11, 2001, represents an epic event in American history, one that compares to the Japanese attack on Pearl Harbor on December 7, 1941. September 11's parallel to Pearl Harbor, however, extends beyond strategic and tactical surprise and the loss of thousands of American lives a few hours after dawn. . . .

As horrific and grievous as the events of September 11 were, that day very easily could have been an even greater catastrophe, one that could have produced, in addition to unprecedented civilian carnage, an unprecedented leadership crisis at the very moment that called for the most vigorous executive leadership, or in Alexander Hamilton's enduring phrase, "energy in the executive."

For one thing, in planning and executing the September 11 attacks, the enemy does not appear to have made decapitating the U.S. government a primary objective. For another, one of the Washington-bound hijacked airliners, United Flight 93, was brought down in a field in Pennsylvania by the heroism of its passengers. But this was made possible only by the unexpected forty-minute delay of that flight's departure from Newark, which allowed the passengers to learn from cell phone calls that their hijackers were bent on a kamikaze mission. The hijacked airliner that did reach Washington, American Flight 77, crashed into the Washington area target singularly capable (as these matters go) of physically absorbing and surviving the blow—the Pentagon. And most important of all, the President—like the aircraft carriers absent from Pearl Harbor on the morning of December 7, 1941—happened to be out of Washington when the enemy struck on September 11.

Thus, the nation was spared an almost unimaginable leadership crisis that could have arisen had the enemy successfully struck the White House and the Capitol on a day when the President was in Washington. Unlike the redundant and relatively reliable mechanisms in place (dating from the Cold War) to ensure continuity in military command and control, the nation's legal arrangements for ensuring the continuity of the Presidency are inadequate and are most likely to fail at precisely the moment when the need for decisive executive authority is most urgent, and when its absence may prove fatal to American lives and interests.

In the event of a vacancy in the Presidency, the 25th Amendment (ratified in 1967 in response to Lyndon Johnson's succession to the Presidency in 1963 following the assassination of President [John F.] Kennedy) is clear: the Vice-President "shall" become President, and the new President "shall" appoint, subject to confirmation by a majority of both houses of Congress, a new Vice President. However, in the event of simultaneous vacancies in the Presidency and the Vice Presidency, or the simultaneous "inability" of these officers to exercise presidential duties, the nation's presidential succession mechanism is probably unconstitutional and is a sure formula for instability, hesitation, and partisan gamesmanship at the worst possible moment. . . .

Compelling Policy Reasons

There are compelling policy reasons against placing the Speaker and the President pro tempore in the line of presidential succession. First, it allows for the possibility that a terrorist attack or some other catastrophe could undo the results of the preceding presidential election by suddenly transferring the Presidency from one party to another. [Terrorist leader] Osama bin Laden should not be permitted to replace the [Democratic Bill] Clinton Administration with the [Republican Speaker of the House Newt] Gingrich Administration, or the [Republican George W.] Bush Administration with the [Democratic president pro tempore of the Senate Robert] Byrd Administration. Presidential succession is traumatic enough when the successor is from the President's own party, as in the case of the assassination of John Kennedy in 1963 or the resignation of Richard Nixon in 1974. The national trauma would be even greater if control of the Executive Branch also changed as a result of assassination or foreign attack. Indeed, the very possibility that a successful attack could result in a change of control of the Presidency (and hence a change in foreign policy) might in certain circumstances even induce foreign enemies to contemplate such an attack, especially if the attack could be passed off as the work of terrorists or domestic madmen.

That the placement of congressional officers in the succession mechanism might be manipulated for partisan purposes was evident during the impeachment of Andrew Johnson [in 1868]. Congress sought to eliminate this possibility with the 1886 Act, but [President] Harry Truman's 1947 Act revived it by reinstating the Speaker and President pro tempore in the line of succession. More recently, after Vice President Spiro Agnew's resignation in 1973, some Democratic members of Congress sought to convince their colleagues to block the confirmation of Gerald Ford to the Vice Presidency, to which Ford had been nominated by President Nixon in the first use of the 25th Amendment, in the expectation that Nixon would ultimately be forced from office [due to his involvement in the Watergate scandal], and that the Presidency would then fall to the Democratic Speaker, Carl Albert, if the Vice Presidency were kept vacant. Fortunately, cooler heads prevailed, and the Democratic-controlled Congress confirmed Ford, but it illustrates the mischief possible under Section 19 [of the 1947 Presidential Succession Act] in the event of a vacancy in the Vice Presidency.

Second, the placement of congressional officers in the line of succession injects partisan tensions into the succession mechanism in other, less obvious ways. For example, on March 30, 1981, while President [Ronald] Reagan was undergoing surgery after suffering a gunshot wound in an assassination attempt, and Vice President George H.W. Bush was aboard Air Force Two returning to Washington from Texas, most of the cabinet convened in the White House Situation Room. From all accounts that have been written of that day, it is clear (and frightening) that Vice President Bush's ability to communicate meaningfully with the White House Situation Room while aboard Air Force Two was marginal at best. . . .

Many Unqualified Officers in Line

Third, as Senator [George] Hoar observed in 1886, history shows that senior cabinet officers such as the Secretary of State and the Secretary of Defense are generally more likely to be better suited to the exercise of presidential duties than legislative officers. The President pro tempore, traditionally the senior member of the party in control of the Senate, may be particularly ill-suited to the exercise of presidential duties due to reasons of health and age, especially in a crisis like September 11 where an Acting President might be called upon to act decisively and even ruthlessly to protect national security.

The Speaker and President pro tempore, however, are not the only statutory successors designated by Section 19 who might lack presidential attributes. In selecting their cabinets, Presidents simply do not exercise the same care that they might exercise in selecting a Vice President, even though under Section 19 any cabinet officer might find himself thrust into the role of Acting President at a moment of supreme crisis comparable to December 7, 1941, and November 22, 1963, rolled into one, which is what September 11, 2001, easily could have been had the President been in Washington and the terrorists been just a bit luckier.

Whether or not they possess presidential attributes, the total number of statutory presidential successors is, at most, seventeen—the Speaker of the House, the President pro tempore of the Senate, and the fifteen members of the cabinet (counting the Secretary of Homeland Security). At any given moment, this number might be reduced by vacancies in these offices, the "inability" of the officers to act, or the ineligibility of some of these officers to assume presidential duties. An example of cabinet officers who are unable to act are those absent from Washington and unable effectively to communicate with Washington, as when several members of John Kennedy's cabinet were on board a jet over the Pacific en route to Japan on November 22, 1963. . . .

Finally, all of the statutory successors work in Washington, D.C., which means, as [political pundit] Norman J. Ornstein has observed, that a nuclear or biological attack on the nation's capital could eliminate the entire line of succession (and the rest of the federal government) in one fell swoop. In that extreme situation, the Presidency would fall (after some period of vacancy) by default into the hands of the surviving representative who convinced his or her surviving colleagues to select him or her as Speaker, or the surviving senator who convinced his or her surviving colleagues to select him or her as President pro tempore. . . .

September 11 aptly demonstrates Sir Winston Churchill's dictum that sometimes in war "the imagination is baffled by the facts." Sooner or later, and perhaps at the hour of maximum national peril, the nation's poorly-designed presidential succession mechanism may plunge the nation into unprecedented political turmoil or deliver the Presidency into the hands of some junior cabinet officer or member of Congress ill-equipped for such a role. The Bush Administration, apparently aware of the potential magnitude of the disaster that might result from simultaneous vacancies in the Presidency and Vice Presidency, took extraordinary steps in the immediate aftermath of September 11 to limit the occasions during which President Bush and Vice President [Dick] Cheney might be found together, at the White House or elsewhere. Indeed, it appears that the Vice President was largely kept away from Washington at an undisclosed "secure location" for several months after September 11, at least when the President was in town.

The Law Should Be Changed

Relocating the Vice President's office to a bunker in the Blue Ridge Mountains is not a permanent or satisfactory solution to the succession problem, especially when the Vice President has important duties of his own, including presiding over a closely-divided Senate where he might be called upon to cast the deciding vote. A better near-term solution is to amend Section 19 to reconstitute the line of succession with officers from those departments with the most important Executive Branch functions and with state governors selected by the President. The Speaker, President pro tempore, and the less important cabinet officers should be removed from the line of presidential succession.

The reconstituted line of succession after the Vice President should begin with the Secretary of State, and continue on with the Secretary of Defense, the Secretary of the Treasury, the Attorney General, and the Secretary of Homeland Security (in that order). These officers should be permitted to exercise presidential duties without resigning their positions, and those officers higher on the list should be able to displace more junior successors only if they had been under a temporary disability at the time the more junior officer accepted presidential duties.

After these cabinet successors, Section 19 should designate as statutory successors those state governors whom the President chooses to "federalize" in their capacity as commanders-in-chief of their states' National Guard. Although the issue is not free from doubt, federalizing a governor in his or her capacity as commander-in-chief of a state's military forces would arguably have the effect of making such a governor an "Officer" of the United States eligible to act as President. (At least it would not be any more unconstitutional than the 1947 Act's placement of congressional officers in the line of succession.) Placing designated "federalized" governors in the line of succession would ensure continuity of the Presidency in the event that all of the cabinet successors were eliminated by an attack on Washington, D.C., with a weapon of mass destruction.

Another possibility is to amend Section 19 to allow the President to nominate, subject to Senate confirmation, a "First Assistant Vice President," "Second Assistant Vice President," and so forth, who would hold these offices and be placed in the line of succession after the principal cabinet officers (or perhaps ahead of them). Although appointment by the President and confirmation by the Senate does not by itself necessarily create the status of "Officer of the United States" for the official so appointed, there is authority that an official empowered by statute to act in the absence or inability of an "Officer of the United States" is necessarily also an "Officer of the United States."

Constitutional Amendment Needed

In the long run, the solution to the problem of the concentration of presidential successors in Washington is a constitutional amendment that allows the President to nominate, subject to Senate confirmation, statutory presidential successors (in addition to the cabinet) who are not "Officers" of the United States, but nevertheless are eminently qualified, to act as President in the extreme situation that the nation would face following the destruction of Washington, D.C., and the elimination of the President, the Vice President, and the statutory cabinet successors. For example, President Bush might nominate former President George H.W. Bush and former Vice President Dan Quayle, both of whom no longer live in Washington, to serve in the line of succession. Similarly, a future Democratic President might nominate former Vice Presidents Al Gore and Walter Mondale to serve in the statutory line of succession.

Such a constitutional amendment, by eliminating the requirement that a statutory successor be an "Officer" of the United States, would also eliminate any doubts about placing state governors in the line of succession, and could provide for succession to the Presidency itself (as opposed to the Acting Presidency). Such a constitutional amendment is necessary to eliminate other uncertainties in the succession mechanism, such as whether the confirmation of a Vice President nominated under the 25th Amendment operates to displace a statutory Acting President who made the nomination. . . .

After the near-miss of September 11, there is no time to lose in ensuring that the presidential succession mechanism is stable, predictable, and seamless, even (and especially) during moments of supreme crisis such as a foreign attack upon the United States.

Presidential Disability Problems Can Be Resolved Without a New Constitutional Amendment

Robert E. Gilbert

Robert E. Gilbert is a professor of political science at Northeastern University in Boston. In the following selection he explains the recommendations of the Working Group on Presidential Disability established by former president Jimmy Carter. This group of about fifty experts, many of whom were physicians, agreed that the Twenty-fifth Amendment does not need revision. They asserted that, although the amendment does not resolve all the potential problems associated with presidential disability, no new amendment could do so either. They believed, however, that guidelines and a formal plan for their implementation are needed, as the amendment has not been invoked in some circumstances envisioned by the amendment's founders. In the group's opinion, determination of presidential impairment is a medical judgment, while determination of inability is a political judgment. The senior physician in the White House should be the source of medical disclosure when impairment is considered under the amendment, and it is the responsibility of the president or designees to make accurate disclosures to the public. Gilbert explains that the Working Group believes that a determination of disability by those closest to the president is most likely to be accepted as legitimate by the public.

Although the Twenty-fifth Amendment offers a remedy for several problems associated with presidential disability, its critics argue that the remedy it offers is indefinite and incomplete. One of these critics is former President Jimmy Carter

Robert E. Gilbert, "The Contemporary Presidency: The Twenty-Fifth Amendment: Recommendations and Deliberations of the Working Group on Presidential Disability," *Presidential Studies Quarterly*, vol. 33, 2003, p. 877. Copyright © 2003 by Center for the Study of the Presidency. Reproduced by permission of Sage Publications.

who, in a 1993 speech and then in a subsequent article, called attention to what he saw as the serious deficiencies of the Twenty-fifth Amendment and who went on to urge the creation of a commission of experts to study these deficiencies and devise a series of solutions. In response to Carter's concerns, the Carter Center [in Atlanta] and the Bowman Gray School of Medicine [now the Wake Forest University School of Medicine in North Carolina] collaborated in establishing the Working Group on Presidential Disability. Because of the research that I have done in this area, I was invited to serve as a member and did so.

The Working Group consisted of approximately 50 persons, a large majority of whom were physicians, including some who had served as White House physicians, several lawyers, including two law school deans, a former U.S. senator who had been the principal architect of the Twenty-fifth Amendment in the 1960s, a few journalists, several staff members from various presidential administrations, and a small number of social scientists. The Group conducted three multiday meetings, the first in January 1993 at the Carter Center (with former President Carter participating), the second in November 1995 at Wake Forest University (with former President [Gerald] Ford participating), and the third in December 1996 at the White House Conference Center, at the end of which the Group's final report and recommendations were presented to President [Bill] Clinton.

Strengths of the Twenty-fifth Amendment

Members of the Working Group quickly agreed that the Twenty-fifth Amendment did not resolve all problems associated with presidential disability, but most members were convinced that no amendment, no matter how detailed it might be, could do so. The vagaries of human pathology and human mortality simply preclude this as even a possibility. Therefore, the sentiment developed rather quickly that an additional amendment or changes to the extant amendment would not be appropriate. Instead, the Working Group determined that the strengths of the amendment should be further enhanced through a number of facilitating mechanisms so that its use would become more regularized and less forbidding. The Working Group's recommendations are as follows:

1. The Twenty-fifth Amendment is a powerful instrument, which delineates the circumstances and methods for succession and transfer of the power of the presidency. It does not require revision or augmentation by another constitutional amendment. However, guidelines are needed to ensure its effective implementation.

2. The Twenty-fifth Amendment has not been invoked in some circumstances envisioned by its founders. When substantial concern about the ability of the president to discharge the powers and duties of office arise, transfer of power under provisions of the Twenty-fifth Amendment should be considered.

3. A formal contingency plan for the implementation of the amendment should be in place before the inauguration of every president.

4. Determination of presidential impairment is a medical judgment based upon evaluation and tests. Close associates, family, and consultants can provide valuable information that contributes to this medical judgment.

5. The determination of presidential inability is a political judgment to be made by constitutional officials.

6. The president should appoint a physician, civil or military, to be senior physician in the White House and to assume responsibility for his or her medical care, direct the Military Medical Unit, and be the source of medical disclosure when considering imminent or existing impairment according to the provisions of the Twenty-fifth Amendment.

7. In evaluating the medical condition of the president, the senior physician in the White House should make use of the best consultants in relevant fields.

8. Balancing the right of the public to be informed regarding presidential illness with the president's right to confidentiality presents dilemmas. While the senior physician to the president is the best source of information about the medical condition of the president, it is the responsibility of the president or designees to make accurate disclosures to the public.

9. The Twenty-fifth Amendment provides a remarkably flexible framework for the determination of presidential inability and the implementation of the transfer of powers. Its provisions should be more widely publicized and its use destigmatized.

Contingency Planning

Most of the Working Group's recommendations are clear and self-explanatory. A few, however, might benefit from elaboration. A case in point is the third, calling for the creation of contingency plans for the amendment's implementation. It was motivated by the fact that the one clear instance in which section 3 of the Twenty-fifth Amendment was not invoked when it should have been came in March 1981 when President [Ronald] Reagan was shot and seriously wounded by a would-be assassin. Despite the fact that the president was described by one of his physicians as being "only five minutes from death" when he arrived at the George Washington University Medical Center and although he was under anesthesia for some three hours, no serious thought was given to invoking the amendment and making Vice President [George H.W.] Bush acting president. Indeed, when White House aides met with Reagan's physicians at the hospital, they never once asked them whether the president's condition justified invocation—or even consideration of invocation. When these aides consulted with Reagan's personal physician, Dr. Daniel Ruge, within the confines of the White House, they failed to raise the issue with him as well. If they had, they would have learned that Dr. Ruge clearly supported invocation. He later said, "there was a period of 10–15 hours when Ronald Reagan was unable to function as President and could not have responded to a crisis. This was the period of time when the Amendment clearly should have been in effect but was not." Although it is unfortunate that section 3 was not utilized in this instance, almost certainly the failure to invoke it was due to the fact that the administration was still in its infancy and had not yet developed procedures relative to the amendment's disability provisions.

The Working Group recommended strongly that such procedures be henceforth developed during the transition period and be in place at the time of inauguration of every new president. It called for the creation of:

> A White House contingency plan which clearly delineates alterations of function, including cognitive, judgmental, behavioral, and communicative capacities, which should cause consideration of a transfer of power. It must define precise lines of authority and communication and specify exact procedures for its execution. It should also include detailed instructions for specific procedures and lines of communication to be followed for implementing the provisions of sections 3 and 4, respectively. . . . Furthermore, the plan should delineate those situations and medical conditions which would normally warrant a voluntary transfer of power under the provisions of Section 3 or an involuntary transfer of power under the provisions of Section 4.

Although such a plan would be classified because it contains highly sensitive information, an unclassified summary, including significant medical aspects, should be released to the public at the beginning of each presidential administration. It is important for the public to understand that the president gave his consent beforehand to the preparation of such a document and that he/she agrees in full with its contents. It is also important that the president's spouse, the aides who would be involved in the implementation of the contingency plan, and the vice president fully understand its terms and regard it as constituting a directive by the president for specific actions to be taken in the event that he/she is unable to carry out the duties of office. For this reason, the plan should specify as clearly and completely as possible the medical conditions and the range of situations that would justify both voluntary and involuntary transfers of power. Once the president approves the contingency plan, his/her physician would thereafter be authorized to release relevant medical information to the vice president and members of the Cabinet whenever an involuntary transfer of power was being contemplated. The president's prior approval would remove any ethical or legal uncertainties concerning the confidentiality of medical information that the White House physician could release to appropriate officials involved in the implementation process of section 4. Former White House physician Lawrence Mohr writes that ". . . this is one of the most important benefits that a contingency plan provides."

The development of such contingency plans has now become somewhat routinized. According to White House physicians associated with George Bush (senior) and Bill Clinton, the contingency plans approved at the start of these administrations set forth scenarios under which invocation of the Twenty-fifth Amendment would be triggered, and established a set of procedures by which medical information would be released to appropriate officials by the senior White House physician. The [George W. Bush] administration has put a similar plan in place. To date, however, no unclassified summary of any of the three administrations' contingency plans has been released to the public, as suggested by the Working Group.

Political Judgments

Two additional recommendations that need to be expanded upon are the fifth, which states that "the determination of presidential inability is a political judgment to be made by constitutional officials" and the seventh, which recommends that "the Senior Physician in the White House should make use of the best consultants in relevant fields." Because these recommendations are intimately related to each other, they will be discussed in tandem. Both of them conform fully to the letter and spirit of the Twenty-fifth Amendment. According to section 4, the officials who determine whether a disabled president should be separated from his/her powers and duties are the vice president and members of the Cabinet, all of whom are constitutional officials. A number of the amendment's critics charge, however, that because these officials owe their high positions to the president, they are unlikely ever to invoke the provisions of section 4, even when they clearly should. This criticism seems quite unwarranted and fails to appreciate the significant benefits brought about by the current constitutional arrangement.

It would, of course, be very difficult for a vice president and Cabinet members to determine to remove their chief from the exercise of power. Vice presidents try hard to avoid being seen as overly ambitious and as grasping at the presidency. They tend instead to be overly deferential and always appear to be loyal to their leader. Cabinet members also must avoid the appearance of being too aggressive. When, for example, Secretary of State Alexander Haig responded to the shooting of Ronald Reagan in March 1981 by stating that he was "in charge" at the White House, his status in Washington with officialdom, the press, and even the president was greatly damaged and he began his descent into political oblivion. But these political facts of life reflect a strength of the amendment rather than a weakness. It should be extraordinarily difficult for the president of the United States to be separated from the powers and duties of office and such action should be contemplated only under the most serious of circumstances.

Additionally, it is precisely because the vice president and Cabinet are so close to the president that their decision to invoke section 4 would likely be accepted by the people as legitimate. A decision to invoke section 4 by those not so close to the president might well be perceived as a coup d'etat. Because a vice president who is acting as president needs legitimacy as he/she carries out the responsibilities of office under unusually difficult circumstances, nothing should be done to undermine such legitimacy. Moreover, because the vice president is elected by the people and Cabinet members are approved for their positions by the people's representatives in the U.S. Senate, a determination of presidential inability by the vice president and Cabinet, with the assistance of highly competent medical consultants in appropriate fields, seems likely to generate the greatest degree of both public and political support for the acting president. . . .

It is precisely because the Twenty-fifth Amendment establishes mechanisms for dealing with a disabled president—while at the same time protecting the institution of the presidency—that gives the amendment its strength. The recommendations of the Working Group on Presidential Disability are designed to build on that strength by allowing for flexibility in the implementation of the amendment's disability procedures and by avoiding proposals that would rigidify those procedures and damage an institution that must be safeguarded. For in a system based on the principles of separation of powers and checks and balances, the problem of a sick presidency dwarfs the problem of a sick president.

The Proposal to Create a Medical Advisory Commission to Determine Presidential Disability Is Fatally Flawed

Robert E. Gilbert

Robert E. Gilbert is a professor of political science at Northeastern University in Boston. In the following viewpoint he argues against the idea of a permanent medical advisory commission that would determine a president's impairment and disability. Such a system, he says, would be a gross governmental intrusion into the medical care received by the president. It would make private information available on a regular basis to untrained and sensationalistic commentators. It would not take into account the fact that there are times when inaction on a president's medical problems would be in the national interest. It might be unconstitutional. Above all, Gilbert continues, it would be damaging to presidents. A president who resisted submitting to examination by such a commission would be accused of a medical cover-up, while one who agreed to it might be badly compromised by its diagnoses and prognoses, which might not be accurate since the physicians on the panel might very well disagree among themselves. By undermining the presidential image of strength, he says, a medical commission would unintentionally undermine the president's ability to lead.

Critics argue that section 4 [of the Twenty-fifth Amendment] is simply not workable, in large part because it requires decisive and overt action against the president by officials who are his subordinates. Given almost no power by the

Robert E. Gilbert, "Psychological Illness in Presidents: A Medical Advisory Commission and Disability Determinations," *Political Psychology*, vol. 27, 2006, pp. 56–63, 72. Copyright © 2006 Basil Blackwell Ltd. Reproduced by permission of Blackwell Publishers.

Constitution, vice presidents tend to be politically weak and vulnerable. Under most circumstances, this makes them quite deferential to their chief and likely to be disinclined to invoke section 4. Cabinet members, who can be fired by the president at will, are likely to be similarly disinclined. However, even if the vice president and Cabinet *were* prepared to invoke section 4, critics argue that they would be deprived of necessary medical information by the White House physician who, as a member of the president's inner circle, would typically conceal the true nature of his/her physical or psychological health. Although [Ronald] Reagan White House Physician Daniel Ruge has indicated that he would have recommended invocation of section 4 after the president was shot in March 1981 if his opinion had been sought, critics cite other presidential physicians from other administrations as having engaged in medical cover-ups. In order to deal with this problem, they offer a complex, highly bureaucratized, and dangerously intrusive solution, one that would be particularly inadequate in assessing psychological impairment.

A Medical Advisory Commission

Although there are variations in the proposals espousing a presidential medical commission, all focus on the establishment of a standing, independent board of physicians that would examine the president once a year and then issue a report of its findings to the vice president, the cabinet, and/or the nation. The originator of one such plan [Herbert Abrams] has recommended that, acting under the authority of a statute or a concurrent resolution of Congress, the surgeon general should appoint a Medical Advisory Commission of six members, including two internists, two neurologists, one surgeon, and one psychiatrist, from a list prepared by the president of the Institute of Medicine of the National Academy of Science and that such members should have overlapping terms of six years. Further, the Commission should include "a reasonable mix of Democrats and Republicans" and its final composition would be "subject to the approval of the Secretary of Health and Human Services." Commission members could not be removed by the president and would serve as a "powerful antidote to the White House cover-ups of the past." Their function would be to "participate in an annual review of pertinent history, systems, physical examination and laboratory data on the president at Walter Reed Hospital or the Naval Medical Center, together with the president's physician" and then communicate their findings to the president, the vice president, and the public. They would also evaluate the president's medical condition whenever the subject of disability arose. The proposal's originator concludes that the existence of such a panel "would preclude inaction by the executive branch in the face of disability."

This proposal is highly problematic. It would set in stone the specific medical specialties represented on the Commission and provide for clearly inadequate representation for mental health specialists. It would represent gross governmental intrusion into the medical care given the president and would interject the president's medical records into the public domain on a regular basis, where they would be analyzed again and again by untrained and sensationalistic commentators—a rather offensive notion in a nation where privacy rights are commonly respected. It would turn the president's annual, full-scale medical examination into a partisan battleground where the administration's friends and foes seek political advantage. It fails to appreciate that there are times when executive branch *inaction* in cases of disability would be in the national interest, as, for example, when a transfer of executive power would cause severe harm in terms of morale and stability. Further, it raises serious issues of constitutionality since, in enacting a statute establishing a formal medical panel for the leader of only one branch of government, Congress might well be violating the Constitution's separation of powers principle.

Apart from the above problems and perhaps more serious than any of them, the establishment of a Medical Advisory Commission would be damaging to presidents. A president who, for any reason, resisted submitting to the examinations of such a group would be suspected and accused of a medical cover-up. A president who agreed to submit to its examinations would likely be badly compromised by its diagnoses and prognoses. Since the physicians serving on such a panel would occasionally—and perhaps often—be in fundamental disagreement with each other, the panel's role in the disability process would be disruptive, making it more difficult for the vice president and cabinet to act, even when they recognized a need to do so. . . .

Differences of Opinion

Differences of opinion among experts are to be expected but they tend to be confusing to nonexperts. Although such disagreements often have significant *legal* ramifications, professional disputes among physicians serving on a Medical Advisory Commission would have potentially devastating *political* effects since the laymen who would be receiving their conflicting and confusing judgments would be in the process of considering whether or not to relieve the president of the United States of his/her powers and duties.

Some proponents of a presidential medical commission try to downplay this problem by arguing that the U.S. Supreme Court is often divided in its decisions and that [according to Abrams] its divided votes "have not shaken the foundations of the republic." But their argument is not persuasive since it ignores the fact that closely divided Supreme Court opinions *are*, in fact, weak and troublesome, particularly when major societal issues are in question. . . .

Closely divided court decisions *have* provoked sharp social discord as seen recently in *Bush v. Gore*. The Court's 5-4 majority in favor of terminating vote recounts in Florida had the effect of giving the 2000 election to Republican candidates [George W.] Bush and [Dick] Cheney, the national popular vote losers. This caused considerable upset throughout the nation. . . .

In matters of presidential disability, it is difficult to believe that the bitterness and controversy that would follow closely divided votes on a Medical Advisory Commission would be in the national interest. In fact, such divided votes would likely precipitate still greater explosions of public outrage than that which followed *Bush v. Gore* since any "removal" of a president, once inaugurated, through "partisan chicanery" would arguably draw even more public fury than his or her inauguration. Although a staunch proponent of a Medical Advisory Commission [namely, Abrams,] has argued that "the independence, breadth of experience, lack of conflict of interest, availability, and credibility of the committee would assure the public of an objective appraisal" of the president's health status, it would, of course, do no such thing. Objectivity often dissipates in the face of partisanship and physicians are likely to be no more objective than judges, or anyone else.

This, in fact, is precisely the charge that proponents of the Medical Commission proposal level against the current arrangement: that White House physicians become so much a part of the inner circle that they make diagnoses and prognoses *subjectively* in order to protect the president *politically*. The same subjectivity might well infuse members of a Medical Advisory Commission, depending on their deep-seated opinion of the president, his/her policies, or party. The possibility that political decision makers might then act—and be pressured to act—on the basis of such subjective judgments is highly disturbing.

It is also important to remember that even a presidential medical commission that was both *unanimous and objective* might simply be incorrect in its diagnosis of the president's physical and psychological health and especially in its prognosis of his/her likely future health status. Therefore, its public intrusion into the political process would be arbitrary and controversial. Any president confronting a damaging assessment by a Medical Advisory Commission would almost certainly move to discredit and refute it by putting together another medical panel that would issue a much more positive prognosis. There would then exist *two* reports on the president's health status, each with quite different conclusions. Contention, partisan conflict, and paralysis would surely ensue—to the country's detriment.

Further, because members of a Medical Advisory Commission would not have nearly as complete an understanding of the president's medical status as his/her regular physicians would be expected to have, their participation in the disability process would represent flawed medical practice....

Psychological Illness

Because the complexities of psychological illness are so varied, a Medical Advisory Commission would be particularly problematic in diagnosing it. First, the manifestations of such illness are often transitory, and sound diagnosis depends not only on access to all sources of clinical information but also on face-to-face human interactions....

A Medical Advisory Commission, operating with only limited access to the president, would be particularly vulnerable to making erroneous judgments. As former Senator Birch Bayh, a principle architect of the 25th Amendment, writes: "Diagnosis of mental illness requires direct observation of the patient and careful consideration of his interactions with other people in various situations. To determine if a president is mentally unable to perform the responsibilities of his office requires continuous diagnosis in the environment in which the president works." Bayh asks whether an impairment panel should "examine the President in the solitude of the oval office, during a vigorous disagreement with Congressional leaders, while Cabinet officers are debating a critical issue, or in the midst of a no-holds-barred press conference?" He concludes that panel members would "not possess the intimate, hour-by-hour, day-to-day knowledge of how a disease affects a given president in the performance of his duties."

Second, in addition to the situational aspects of psychological illness described above, the signs of such illness may be heightened or diminished by season of the year, usually worse in the fall and winter and better in the spring, and even by ambient light levels. They may be affected, too, by the time of day during which a person is observed. . . .

Third, people exhibit occasional and temporary symptoms of mental illness, ranging from feeling "blue" to a mood of enthusiasm approaching manic proportions. Individuals with schizoaffective disorders experience the presence of such mood episodes for a period of time but not all the time. . . .

The differentiating characteristics of these conditions are important because quite different levels of functional ability attach to each. This, of course, is a vital consideration when invocations of the 25th Amendment are being contemplated. Yet, it is unlikely that a Medical Advisory Commission could effectively decide among diagnoses of schizophrenia, schizofrenoform disorder, or brief psychotic disorder since its time with the president would be so limited. . . .

Fourth, limited interaction with a patient almost certainly increases the tendency of clinicians to engage in confirmatory bias. They might, in other words, seek and rely on evidence that supports their own predispositions rather than evidence that runs contrary to them. . . .

Fifth, sharp differences of opinion exist within the mental health community over the diagnostic criteria established by the American Psychiatric Association for diagnosing the symptoms of mental illness. . . . The possibility that diagnoses of mental illnesses could be shaped by political considerations is chilling, particularly within the context of determining presidential disability. . . .

Even given a diagnosis of schizophrenia or paranoia, how schizophrenic must a president be before section 4 of the 25th Amendment should be invoked? How paranoid? It is very doubtful that panel members who saw the president once a year would be able to make such a judgment with confidence. It is equally doubtful that political decision makers would then put trust in the judgments they offered—or that they should.

A sixth major problem associated with psychological illness is that symptoms may be regarded as not at all problematic by the "patient" and may be masked. In the case of the president of the United States, this would not only be understandable, given the fear of public backlash, but could also make diagnosis very difficult, even for his personal physician. . . .

The Presidential Image

The 25th Amendment is intended to safeguard the country from instances of physical and/or psychological disability in presidents. Yet the mechanisms by which such disability is determined must be *medically and politically* appropriate and not have unintended detrimental consequences. Dr. Rudolph Marx reminds us that especially in psychological examinations, "the borderline between the realms of sickness and health are indefinite and fluid, and subject to arbitrary interpretation. . . ." In order to minimize such arbitrariness, a sustained period of close observation between doctor and patient is essential. A Medical Advisory Commission fails badly in providing such sustained interaction and, therefore, would almost certainly increase the likelihood of arbitrary and capricious medical judgments, thereby dangerously impairing the disability process itself.

Further, since the public expects its president to be strong and in control, presidential image—vitally important to presidential leadership—must be safe-guarded. By compromising the image of presidential strength and projecting instead the image of presidential weakness and vulnerability, a Medical Commission, no matter how unintentionally, would undermine the president's ability to lead and thereby erode presidential power. Particularly is this true in the assessment of psychological illness where public fear and misunderstanding are still so prevalent. Few would follow a president whose psychological health was called into question. The proposal for a Medical Advisory Commission, then, is fatally flawed.

Appendix

Appendix

The Amendments to the U.S. Constitution

Amendment I: Freedom of Religion, Speech, Press, Petition, and Assembly (ratified 1791)

Amendment II: Right to Bear Arms (ratified 1791)

Amendment III: Quartering of Soldiers (ratified 1791)

Amendment IV: Freedom from Unfair Search and Seizures (ratified 1791)

Amendment V: Right to Due Process (ratified 1791)

Amendment VI: Rights of the Accused (ratified 1791)

Amendment VII: Right to Trial by Jury (ratified 1791)

Amendment VIII: Freedom from Cruel and Unusual Punishment (ratified 1791)

Amendment IX: Construction of the Constitution (ratified 1791)

Amendment X: Powers of the States and People (ratified 1791)

Amendment XI: Judicial Limits (ratified 1795)

Amendment XII: Presidential Election Process (ratified 1804)

Amendment XIII: Abolishing Slavery (ratified 1865)

Amendment XIV: Equal Protection, Due Process, Citizenship for All (ratified 1868)

The Amendments to the U.S. Constitution

Amendment XV: Race and the Right to Vote (ratified 1870)
Amendment XVI: Allowing Federal Income Tax (ratified 1913)
Amendment XVII: Establishing Election to the U.S. Senate
                   (ratified 1913)
Amendment XVIII: Prohibition (ratified 1919)
Amendment XIX: Granting Women the Right to Vote (ratified 1920)
Amendment XX: Establishing Term Commencement for Congress
                   and the President (ratified 1933)
Amendment XXI: Repeal of Prohibition (ratified 1933)
Amendment XXII: Establishing Term Limits for U.S. President
                   (ratified 1951)
Amendment XXIII: Allowing Washington, D.C., Representation in the
                   Electoral College (ratified 1961)
Amendment XXIV: Prohibition of the Poll Tax (ratified 1964)
Amendment XXV: Presidential Disability and Succession
                   (ratified 1967)
Amendment XXVI: Lowering the Voting Age (ratified 1971)
Amendment XXVII: Limiting Congressional Pay Increases
                   (ratified 1992)

For Further Research

Books

Herbert L. Abrams, *The President Has Been Shot: Confusion, Disability, and the 25th Amendment.* Stanford, CA: Stanford University Press, 1994.

Birch Bayh, *One Heartbeat Away: Presidential Disability and Succession.* Indianapolis: Bobbs-Merrill, 1968.

Continuity of Government Commission, *Preserving Our Institutions: Presidential Succession.* Washington, DC: AEI-Brookings Continuity of Government Commission, 2009.

Kenneth R. Crispell and Carlos Gomez, *Hidden Illness in the White House.* Durham, NC: Duke University Press, 1988.

John D. Feerick, *From Failing Hands: The Story of Presidential Succession.* New York: Fordham University Press, 1965.

————, *The Twenty-Fifth Amendment: Its Complete History and Earliest Application.* New York: Fordham University Press, 1992.

Robert H. Ferrell, *Ill-Advised: Presidential Health and Public Trust.* Columbia: University of Missouri Press, 1992.

Gerald R. Ford, *A Time to Heal.* New York: Harper and Row, 1979.

Robert E. Gilbert, *The Mortal Presidency: Illness and Anguish in the White House.* New York: Fordham University Press, 1998.

————, ed., *Managing Crisis: Presidential Disability and the 25th Amendment.* New York: Fordham University Press, 2000.

Davis S. Houck, *FDR's Body Politics: The Rhetoric of Disability.* College Station: Texas A&M University Press, 2003.

Phyllis Lee Levin, *Edith and Woodrow: The Wilson White House*. New York: Scribner, 2001.

Rose McDermott, *Presidential Leadership, Illness, and Decision Making*. New York: Cambridge University Press, 2008.

Lester A. Sobel, ed., *Presidential Succession: Ford, Rockefeller and the 25th Amendment*. New York: Facts On File, 1975.

Kenneth W. Thompson, ed., *Papers on Presidential Disability and the Twenty-fifth Amendment*. 4 vols. Lanham, MD: University Press of America and Miller Center of Public Affairs, University of Virginia, 1988–97.

James F. Toole and Robert J. Joynt, eds., *Presidential Disability: Papers, Discussions, and Recommendations on the Twenty-fifth Amendment and Issues of Inability and Disability Among Presidents of the United States*. Rochester, NY: University of Rochester, 2001.

Periodicals

Herbert L. Abrams, "The One Who Can't Get Sick," *New York Times*, March 31, 1981.

Richard V. Allen, "The Day Reagan Was Shot," *Atlantic*, April 2001.

Lawrence K. Altman, "The Doctor's World: Many Holes in Disclosure of Nominees' Health," *New York Times*, October 20, 2008.

———, "The Doctor's World: Very Real Questions for Fictional President," *New York Times*, October 9, 2001.

———, "Presidential Power: Reagan Doctor Says He Erred," *New York Times*, February 20, 1989.

Birch Bayh, "The White House Safety Net," *New York Times*, April 8, 1995.

Elizabeth Bumiller, "Bush to Undergo Colon Procedure," *New York Times*, June 29, 2002.

James MacGregor Burns, "Let's Stop Gambling with the Presidency," *Saturday Evening Post*, January 25, 1964.

Linda Charlton, "25th Amendment: Its Critics Say Amend or Abandon It; the Rockefeller Hearings Prompt Renewed Discussion," *New York Times*, November 17, 1974.

Michelle Cottle, "Norman Ornstein's Doomsday Scenario," *Atlantic*, June 2003.

Gerald R. Ford, "The Path Back to Dignity," *New York Times*, October 4, 1998.

Michael J. Halberstam, "Who's Medically Fit for the White House? A Doctor Says It's Too Important to Be Left to the Doctors," October 22, 1972.

Michael Janofsky, "The Many Ailments of the Presidents," *New York Times*, November 4, 1996.

Ashby Jones, "Who Reigns in Succession Crisis? Confusion, Perhaps," *Wall Street Journal*, November 13, 2008.

Wayne King and Warren Weaver, "Briefing: On Presidential Disability," *New York Times*, March 30, 1986.

James Mann, "The Armageddon Plan," *Atlantic*, March 2004.

Bill Marsh, "When the Vice President Really Matters," *New York Times*, September 7, 2008.

James M. McNaughton, "Ford Backs Reappraisal of Presidential Succession," *New York Times*, February 27, 1975.

Herbert Mitgang, "Books of the Times: America's Big Built-in Gamble," *New York Times*, March 10, 1992.

Robert L. Noland, "Presidential Disability and the Proposed Constitutional Amendment," *American Psychologist*, March 1966.

Norman Ornstein, "It's Armageddon: Who's in Charge Here?" *Fortune*, February 9, 2004.

———, "Unprepared: Why Inauguration Day Is Dangerous," *New Republic*, January 17, 2005.

Howell Raines, "By a Pause, Then Government Moves Ahead," *New York Times*, April 5, 1981.

William Safire, "Ignoring Section 4," *New York Times*, June 6, 1983.

Arthur Schlesinger Jr., "Taking the 25th," *New York Times*, October 3, 1973.

Beverly Smith Jr., "If a President Collapses," *Saturday Evening Post*, March 28, 1957.

Richard Stengel, "Who's Minding the Store?" *Time*, April 12, 2005.

Stuart Taylor Jr., "Disabling of Reagan Provokes a Debate over Nuclear Authority in Such Cases," *New York Times*, April 4, 1981.

———, "Reagan's Illness: Governmental Questions; Power Transfer Seen as Precedent," *New York Times*, July 16, 1985.

Warren Weaver, "Law Experts Critical of 25th Amendment," *New York Times*, December 20, 1974.

Steven R. Weisman, "White House Aides Assert Weinberger Was Upset When Haig Took Charge," *New York Times*, April 1, 1981.

Tom Wicker, "Near Miss for Ford and U.S.," *New York Times*, September 9, 1975.

Internet Resources

Akhil Reed Amar and Vikram David Amar, "Presidency: What the 25th Amendment Overlooks," History News Network, August 12, 2002. http://hnn.us/articles/902.html.

Matthew Coleman, "Ford Talks on Presidential Disability," *Old Gold and Black*, Wake Forest University, November 16, 1995. http://ogb.wfu.edu/back_issues/1995_Fall/11-16-95/News/n.ford.html.

Larry Diamond, "Terrorism: Preparing for the Worst," *Hoover Digest*, 2002. www.hoover.org/publications/digest/3437 261.html.

John C. Fortier, "*The West Wing* and Presidential Succession: Fact or Fiction?" American Enterprise Institute for Public Policy, September 24, 2003. www.aei.org/article/19238.

Geoffrey D. Garin, "Choice of Agnew's Successor Subject to 25th Amendment," *Harvard Crimson*, October 10, 1973. www.thecrimson.com/article.aspx?ref=180349.

Steve Mount, "Constitutional Topic: Presidential Disability," U.S. Constitution Online, March 15, 2006. www.usconstitution.net/consttop_pdis.html.

Senate Judiciary Committee, "Ensuring the Continuity of the United States Government: The Presidency," September 16, 1993. http://judiciary.senate.gov/hearings/hearing .cfm?id=914.

Peter M. Shane, "Torturing the Twenty-fifth," TPM Cafe, April 7, 2007. http://tpmcafe.talkingpointsmemo.com/2007/04/ 07/25th_amendment_revisited_via_t.

Web Sites

Amendment 25, http://amendment25.com. A compendium of information about the Twenty-fifth Amendment and the presidential succession law, including their history and their use in fiction.

American Presidency Project, www.presidency.ucsb.edu. A collection of historical documents, including a few related to the Twenty-fifth Amendment.

Archives Library Information Center, www.archives.gov/
research/alic/reference/presidents.html#25. An official site
of the U.S. National Archives. The site contains a few
documents related to the Twenty-fifth Amendment.

Continuity of Government Commission, www.continuityof
government.org. A commission launched in the fall of
2002 to study and recommend reforms to ensure the continuity of U.S. governmental institutions in the event of a
catastrophic attack. It studies presidential succession,
among other topics.

Vice Presidents.org, www.vicepresidents.org. Web magazine
on the vice presidency of the United States, containing
biographies, stories, trivia, history, and commentary about
all the vice presidents.

Index

A

Abrams, Herbert, 143, 183

Abzug, Bella, 87

Acting president
Cheney as, 124, 128
constitutional provision for, 75–76
forfeit of previous office by, 154–155
interim leadership by, 146
invocation of Twenty-fifth Amendment by, 110
Secretary of State as, 136
Speaker of the House as, 110–111, 137
vice president as, 19, 37, 41–43, 48–53, 118, 125–126, 128

Adams, John Quincy, 19

Agnew, Spiro, 22, 79, 128–129, 168

Albert, Carl, *93*, 168

Allen, Richard V., 132

Amar, Akhil Reed, 124–129, 153

Amar, Vikram David, 124–129

Anesthesia, transfer of power during, 23, 98–107, 124, 143

Arkin, William M., 130–133

Arthur, Chester A., 20, 46–47, 74, 127

Assassination
attempted, of Reagan, 95–97, 168–169, 177–178
of Garfield, 19–20, 45–46, 66, 74, 126–127
of Kennedy, 19–21, 55, 63, 131, 167

Associated Press, 104–107

B

Baker, M. Miller, 153, 165–173

Bayh, Birch
on caretaker vice president, 80
debate over Twenty-fifth Amendment and, 23, 76, 113–114
introduction of Twenty-fifth Amendment by, 21
on mental illness, 187

Bill of Rights, 67

Blaine, James G., 45, 46

Brownell, Herbert, Jr., 122

Bumping procedure, 153–155, 160

Burns, James MacGregor, 19

Bush, George H.W.
during assassination attempt on Reagan, 168–169, 177
transfer of power to, by Reagan, 95–97, 98–103, 115–117

Bush, George W., invocation of Twenty-fifth Amendment by, 23, 104–107, 124, 128

Bush v. Gore (2000), 185–186

C

Cabinet
line of succession and, 34, 57–58, 160–162, 169–171
questions of presidential disability and, 39, 114, 180–181

Cannon, Howard, 82

Carter, Jimmy, 174–175

Cheney, Dick
nuclear weapons and, 132
after September 11, 2001, 170